LEARN
TO COOK
WITH
NEVEN

LEARN TO COOK WITH NEVEN

NEVEN MAGUIRE

GILL BOOKS

Gill Books
Hume Avenue
Park West
Dublin 12
www.gillbooks.ie

Gill Books is an imprint of M.H. Gill and Co.

© Neven Maguire 2021

978 0717 19262 5

Compiled by Orla Broderick
Designed by www.grahamthew.com
Photographed by Joanne Murphy (www.joanne-murphy.com)
Styled by Chloe Chan
Prop styling by Chloe Chan and Joanne Murphy
Assistants: Susan Will and Anna Colwell
Copy-edited by Kristin Jensen
Indexed by Eileen O'Neill
Printed by L.E.G.O. SpA, Italy

DEDICATION

For our twins, Connor and Lucia, and everyone who is enjoying learning to cook at home. I hope this book will bring a lot of pleasure and fun in the kitchen for years to come.

ACKNOWLEDGEMENTS

This has been a year like no other. But it has given me the opportunity to be at home, to be with my family more than I ever have before, and to spend precious time with Amelda, Connor and Lucia.

I wrote this book when we were in lockdown. Yes, it was a strange time for everyone, but in the Maguire house we had great fun creating and enjoying these recipes. There are no better critics than Connor and Lucia!

Some of these recipes are ones that went down well on our Zoom demos. This could not have been possible without the help of Amelda; she is a wonderful camera lady! She not only has a steady hand for the camera but is a steady support to me. I could not do what I do without her.

Once again it was a pleasure to work with Gill Books, and I want to thank the whole Gill Books team, in particular Nicki Howard. I want to sincerely thank Orla Broderick, who has helped me with all the recipes for all my books. Her attention to detail is unique. Thanks to Chloe Chan for the delicious food-styling and finally to Joanne Murphy for taking such beautiful photographs.

Eating with family and enjoying home-cooked meals with the very best of Irish produce is of the utmost importance in our family. This is something that I learned from my mum and dad. For me, getting your children to cook is one of the greatest gifts we can give them. Thanks to the Bord Bia team, especially Hylda Adams, for the cook-along campaign. I have the opportunity to cook with children of all ages, and there is no better skill to teach our future adults than to be able to produce delicious, home-cooked food for friends and family.

Amelda and I have been thrilled to see Connor and Lucia getting interested in the kitchen. Who knows where it will take them? If they cook at home with their families in time, I will be more than happy.

As always, I thank everyone who continues to support me in my life.

Enjoy your kitchen, the heart of the house.

CONTENTS

DINNER

BAKING & TREATS

THE ULTIMATE GUIDE TO KITCHEN SKILLS

INTRODUCTION

I GOT THE love of cooking from my mum, Vera, and from my Auntie Maureen. I still use some of their recipes today. I started out with baking. Begin with things like flapjacks, shortbread and apple tart, things that aren't difficult to cook and that you can enjoy eating straight away. I used to make a big mess in the kitchen. My children do the same now and I love it!

My mother quickly took me under her wing, taking the time to show me all the tips and tricks for making delicious homemade food. As you know I went on to become a chef and have loved every minute of it. But most people aren't going to choose it as a career. My three brothers and four sisters are all excellent cooks, but each of them took different paths in life. Even so, they have all been able to enjoy home-cooked meals with their families and that, to me, is one of the real pleasures of food – eating tasty, nutritious meals with family and friends. That's why I think that learning to cook is one of the most important skills you can have. We all need to eat food every day, so why not learn to cook and eat well? If I hadn't become a chef I would still appreciate the introduction to food that I was so lucky to receive.

My job has taken me all around the world learning about food cultures in places like Thailand, Vietnam, Italy, the USA and Spain, where I just filmed my latest TV show. There is still always so much to learn. And that is how I think of this book. There are lots of recipes that you can try and there will then be the opportunity to improve and vary them each time you go back to them. Some of these will, I hope, be meals that you will enjoy throughout your life.

In Ireland, we have some of the best food in the world available to us. Our farmers and artisan producers are second to none. If I can give you just one tip, it's this: if you use the very best ingredients, you won't go far wrong.

I hope this book encourages you to spend some happy times in the kitchen chopping, stirring, frying and baking to create some wonderful food experiences for you, your friends and your family. There are many happy memories just waiting to be made.

Take a picture of your creations and send them to me. I'd love to see how you get on.

Until then, happy cooking!

Neven

BREAKFAST

DIPPY EGGS WITH SOLDIERS

The eggshells are less likely to crack if the eggs are at room temperature. Try to use organic eggs for this recipe, as their yolks have the most beautiful soft yellow colour.

Serves 1

- 2 large eggs
- 2 slices of wholegrain bread
- knob of butter
- pinch of salt

1

Bring a pan of water to the boil over a medium heat. Gently lower in the eggs on a spoon. Put on a timer and cook for 5 minutes for a runny yolk or up to 7 for a more set but still spoonable yolk.

2

Meanwhile, toast the bread and spread with butter, then cut into soldiers.

3

Carefully lift out the eggs with a tongs and put into egg cups.

4

Using a teaspoon, crack off the tops and season with a pinch of salt. Put the dippy eggs on a plate with the toast soldiers to serve.

BUTTERMILK PANCAKES

These are the real deal – the lightest, puffiest, American-style pancakes you can imagine thanks to the buttermilk. Apple syrup is Ireland's answer to maple syrup. It's produced by Highbank Orchards in Kilkenny and can be bought under the Simply Better range at Dunnes Stores or in other good shops.

Makes 6

- 100g (4oz) plain flour
- 1 tsp baking powder
- good pinch of sea salt
- 1 large egg
- 6 tbsp buttermilk
- rapeseed oil, for frying
- 4 tbsp thick Greek-style yoghurt
- 2–4 tsp apple syrup

1
Heat a non-stick frying pan over a medium heat. Place the flour, baking powder and salt in a bowl and mix to combine.

2
Make a well in the centre. Break in the egg and add the buttermilk, then whisk until smooth.

3
Add enough oil to just coat the heated pan. Using a ladle, add about 3 tablespoons of batter for each pancake. Cook three pancakes at a time for 1–2 minutes, until tiny bubbles appear, then flip over and cook for 1–2 minutes, until golden.

4
Stack onto warm plates and add a dollop of yoghurt to each one, then drizzle over the apple syrup to serve.

OMELETTE FLORENTINE

The secret to a light, fluffy omelette is to barely whisk the eggs and to only do it as you are heating the pan. The omelette continues to cook once it has left the pan, so cook it until you can still see a little runniness in the middle before adding the filling.

Makes 1

- 2 eggs
- 2 tsp softened butter
- handful of baby spinach leaves
- 1 tbsp freshly grated Parmesan cheese
- sea salt and freshly ground black pepper

1
Heat a non-stick frying pan over a medium heat. Break the eggs into a bowl and season lightly with salt and pepper, then lightly beat with a fork.

2
Add the butter to the heated pan and gently swirl until it melts and coats the bottom. Add the eggs and repeat the gentle swirling motion so that the eggs are in an even layer.

3
Using a spatula, stir the egg mixture just once in a figure of eight. Cook for about 2 minutes, until the eggs are set and the edges look a little crisp and golden.

4
Scatter the spinach leaves over one half of the omelette, then sprinkle the Parmesan on top. Using the spatula, fold the omelette in half and slide onto a plate to serve.

HAMBLED EGGS WITH AVO & TOMATOES

These ham-scrambled eggs are pillowy and fluffy, certain to make your morning bright! The trick is to leave the mixture long enough to form large curds, which my twins, Connor and Lucia, seem to prefer to regular scrambled eggs.

Serves 2

- 2 cherry tomato vines
- 3 tsp rapeseed oil
- 4 eggs
- 1 tbsp cream
- 50g (2oz) cooked ham, shredded
- 1 ripe avocado
- sea salt and freshly ground black pepper

1
Preheat the oven to 190°C (375°F/gas mark 5). Put the cherry tomatoes in a baking tin and drizzle with 1 teaspoon of the oil. Season with salt and pepper and roast in the oven for 15 minutes.

2
Heat a non-stick frying pan over a low heat. Break the eggs into a bowl and add the cream, then season with salt and pepper. Beat lightly with a fork. Add the remaining 2 teaspoons of oil to the pan and swirl it around.

3
Add the egg mixture and leave to cook for 30 seconds, then stir with a spatula into the centre of the pan so that large curds begin to form. Scatter over the ham and stir every 30 seconds, until almost all the liquid has turned into curds.

4
Cut the avocado in half and remove the stone, then peel and cut into slices. Arrange on plates with the hambled eggs and cherry tomatoes and season with a little more salt and pepper to serve.

EGGY BREAD BLT

Eggy bread, aka French toast, made into a sandwich with one of my favourite fillings – what's not to like? The eggy bread could also be drizzled with apple syrup and scattered with your favourite fruit, but for me there is something particularly delicious about this savoury version.

Serves 2

- 2 eggs
- 1 tbsp milk
- 1 small ciabatta loaf
- about 4 tsp rapeseed oil
- 2 rindless bacon rashers
- 2 tsp mayonnaise
- 1 tsp Dijon mustard
- 1 tbsp tomato ketchup
- 2 tomatoes, thinly sliced
- 25g (1oz) Little Gem lettuce leaves
- sea salt and freshly ground black pepper

1

Crack the eggs into a shallow dish. Add the milk, season and beat with a fork. Cut the ciabatta in half lengthwise, then cut in half again across the width. Place cut side down in the egg mixture and leave to soak for 1 minute before turning.

2

Heat a large frying pan over a medium heat and add half the oil. Add the bases, cut side down, pressing with a metal slice. Cook for 2 minutes, until golden, then turn over and cook for 2 minutes. Remove from the pan and repeat with the tops.

3

Meanwhile, preheat the grill. Arrange the bacon on a grill rack and cook for a couple of minutes on each side, until really crispy. Keep warm.

4

Mix together the mayonnaise and mustard. Spread the ketchup on the bases, then add the tomato and season. Top with the lettuce and bacon. Spread the Dijon mayonnaise on the tops of the eggy bread. Sandwich together to serve.

SWEETCORN CAKES WITH SALSA

Whisking the egg white helps to make these as light as a feather! You could use grated carrot or courgette instead of the sweetcorn if you prefer. A good tip is to use scissors to thinly slice the spring onions, as it's easier than using a knife.

Serves 2

- 50g (2oz) semolina or quick polenta
- ½ tsp bicarbonate of soda
- pinch of ground cumin
- 1 large egg
- 150g (5oz) sweetcorn kernels (thawed if frozen or use canned)
- 2 spring onions, very finely chopped
- 4 tbsp thick Greek-style yoghurt
- 2 tbsp rapeseed oil
- 1 tomato, finely chopped
- 1 small red onion, finely chopped
- 1 tsp apple cider vinegar
- sea salt and freshly ground black pepper

1

Put the semolina or polenta, bicarbonate of soda, cumin and a pinch of salt into bowl. Stir to combine and make a well in the centre.

2

Separate the egg and put the yolk in the semolina mixture. Put the egg white into another bowl and set aside. Add the sweetcorn, spring onions, yoghurt and 1 tablespoon of the oil to the semolina mixture, then beat hard to form a smooth batter.

3

Heat a large frying pan over a medium heat. Whisk the egg white to soft peaks and fold into the batter. Add 1 teaspoon of oil to the pan. Ladle in 2 tablespoons of batter for each cake and cook for 3 minutes on each side, until golden brown. Repeat.

4

Mix the tomato in a bowl with the red onion and vinegar. Season generously and stir in the rest of the oil. Arrange the sweetcorn cakes on plates with the tomato salsa to serve.

SAUSAGE & EGG BLAA

Pot roasting sausages is a clever way to cook them. Try to choose ones with a high meat content – I get mine from a Bord Bia Quality Assured butcher where I live in Blacklion in Co. Cavan. That means you know that the meat is Irish and very good quality.

Serves 2

- 2 thick sausages
- 2 tsp rapeseed oil
- 2 eggs
- 2 Waterford blaas (soft floury baps)
- 2 tsp Ballymaloe relish or tomato ketchup
- sea salt and freshly ground black pepper

1
Preheat the oven to 180°C (350°F/gas mark 4). Place the sausages in a cast iron frying pan or small baking tin and roast in the oven for 20 minutes, until cooked through and golden brown.

2
After 15 minutes, heat a non-stick frying pan over a medium heat and add the oil. Crack in the eggs, then season and cook for 2 minutes. Flip over and cook for 1 minute.

3
Meanwhile, split the Waterford blaas. Unless you've bought them fresh on the day, you might need to lightly toast them on a baking sheet in the oven for 2 minutes.

4
Remove the sausages from the oven and leave to rest for a few minutes, then cut each one in half lengthwise, using a fork to keep them steady. Spread the blaa bottoms with the relish or ketchup. Top with the egg, sausages and blaa tops.

SOUFFLÉ EGGS WITH SOURDOUGH

Normally you would need to make a white sauce (called béchamel) to make a soufflé, and of course you still can, but this recipe uses a brilliant shortcut with a carton of fresh cheese sauce available in all good supermarkets.

Serves 4

- knob of butter
- 25g (1oz) fresh ciabatta breadcrumbs
- 6 eggs
- 1 x 350g (12oz) carton of fresh cheese sauce
- sea salt and freshly ground black pepper
- sourdough toast, to serve

1

Preheat the oven to 180°C (350°F/ gas mark 4). Put a baking sheet on the middle shelf. Butter a 20cm (8in) cast iron frying pan or similar, then sprinkle in the breadcrumbs to coat evenly. Tip out any excess.

2

Separate the eggs, carefully putting the whites in one large bowl and the yolks in a separate large bowl. Stir the cheese sauce into the yolks and season with salt and pepper.

3

Whisk the egg whites until peaks form that just hold their shape (an electric whisk is the easiest option). Using a metal spoon, gently fold the whites into the cheese mixture in a figure eight.

4

Spoon the mixture into the prepared frying pan, then run a cutlery knife around the edge to help the soufflé to rise. Place on a baking sheet and bake for 25–30 minutes, until golden but still with a slight wobble. Serve with the toast.

PEANUT BUTTER & JELLY WAFFLES

You don't need a waffle iron for this recipe, only a griddle pan! It works so well – just leave enough room so that they are easy to flip. The less you have to stir the batter once you've added the melted butter, the lighter and fluffier your waffles will be.

Serves 4

- 500g (1lb 2oz) strawberries, plus extra to serve
- juice of 1 small lemon
- 2 tbsp apple syrup or honey
- 100g (4oz) butter
- 225g (8oz) self-raising flour
- 2 tsp baking powder
- pinch of salt
- 2 large eggs
- 300ml (½ pint) buttermilk
- 1 tsp vanilla extract
- 2 tbsp sunflower oil
- 6 tbsp smooth peanut butter

1 First make the strawberry 'jelly'. Put the strawberries, lemon juice and apple syrup or honey in a pan over a medium-high heat. Bring to the boil, then reduce the heat and simmer until the strawberries have broken down and the sauce has thickened.

2 Melt the butter in a pan or in the microwave and cool. Sieve the flour, baking powder and salt into a large bowl. Make a well in the centre and crack in the eggs, then pour in the buttermilk and vanilla. Whisk to combine, then stir in the melted butter.

3 Place a griddle pan over a high heat. Brush with oil, then add enough batter to make three small waffles. Reduce the heat to medium-low and cook for 4–5 minutes, until golden brown. Flip over and cook for 1–2 minutes to crisp up. Repeat.

4 Beat the peanut butter in a bowl to loosen it into a smooth sauce. Arrange the waffles on plates or a platter with the peanut sauce and jelly. Serve with extra strawberries.

LUCIA'S PINK PORRIDGE

What little girl doesn't love pink and this porridge is pretty enough to paint! Packed full of goodness with a sneaky glug of beetroot juice to make the colour pop, they'll be none the wiser ... or of course you can leave it out altogether.

Serves 4

- 100g (4oz) porridge oats
- 300ml (½ pint) milk
- 150ml (¼ pint) water
- 225g (8oz) mixed berries (such as raspberries, blueberries and halved blackberries)
- finely grated rind and juice of ½ lemon
- 1 tsp balsamic vinegar
- 4 tbsp apple syrup or honey
- 100g (4oz) strawberries, hulled
- 3–4 tbsp apple and beetroot juice (Ballyhoura Apple Farm makes a great one)
- 50g (2oz) pecan nuts, chopped

1 Place the oats, milk and water in a bowl. Combine the berries, lemon rind and juice, balsamic vinegar and 2 tablespoons of the apple syrup or honey in a separate bowl. Cover both with clingfilm and chill in the fridge overnight.

2 The next morning, pour the porridge mixture into a heavy-based pan. Bring to the boil, then reduce the heat and simmer for 8–10 minutes, until thickened, stirring all the time.

3 Add the strawberries, beetroot juice and the remaining 2 tablespoons of apple syrup or honey. Using a hand-held blender, blitz until smooth.

4 Spoon the pink porridge into shallow bowls and decorate with the marinated berries and pecans to serve.

CONNOR'S GRANOLA

This recipe is so easy to make and it's a favourite of my son, Connor. Seed and trail mixes are available in the supermarkets and they save you having to buy lots of different packets that are in danger of lingering in the cupboard. This recipe simply uses one packet of each.

Fills a 600ml (1 pint) Kilner jar

- 4 tbsp sunflower oil
- 4 tbsp honey
- 350g (12oz) porridge oats
- 100g (4oz) seed mix (pumpkin, sesame, chia)
- 100g (4oz) trail mix (raisins, honey roasted peanuts, pineapple and cranberries)
- natural yoghurt, banana, raspberries and blueberries, to serve

1
Preheat the oven to 160°C (325°F/gas mark 3). Line a baking sheet with non-stick baking paper.

2
Put the oil and honey in a large pan over a low heat and stir until they have melted together. Stir in the oats and the seed mix until evenly combined, then tip out onto the lined baking sheet. Bake for 20–25 minutes, until golden.

3
Stir in the trail mix and leave to cool, then transfer to a Kilner jar or suitable airtight container until ready to use.

4
To serve, put some granola into a serving bowl and top with a dollop of yoghurt. Slice up a banana and scatter some raspberries and blueberries on top.

NUTTY APPLE BIRCHER MUESLI

Con Traas owns the Apple Farm in Tipperary, where apples have been grown for hundreds of years. He's been championing Irish apple varieties since I've known him and has worked hard to get them on our supermarket shelves. Next time you're shopping, read the labels and buy the Irish ones.

Serves 4

- 1 Irish eating apple, such as Elstar
- 100g (4oz) porridge oats
- 25g (1oz) shredded coconut
- 4 tbsp raisins
- 1 tbsp apple syrup or honey, plus extra to serve
- 1 tsp vanilla extract
- 300ml (½ pint) milk (or use almond, oat or hazelnut milk if you prefer)
- 50g (2oz) shelled pistachios
- 6 tbsp thick Greek-style natural yoghurt

1
Grate the apple, discarding the core, and place in a large bowl.

2
Add the oats, coconut, raisins, apple syrup or honey and vanilla, then pour in the milk. Mix well to combine. Cover with clingfilm and chill overnight.

3
Cut the pistachio nuts into slivers.

4
Spoon the bircher muesli into bowls and add a dollop of the yoghurt to each one. Drizzle over extra apple syrup or honey and scatter the pistachio slivers on top to serve.

BERRY GOOD START SMOOTHIE BOWL

The fun in making a smoothie bowl is in the decoration – approach it like you're painting a picture, but most importantly, have fun doing it. I often freeze summer berries when they're bursting with flavour, then use them throughout the year in recipes like this.

Serves 2

- 2 small bananas
- 225g (8oz) frozen Irish mixed berries (blackberries, raspberries and blackcurrants)
- 6 tbsp natural yoghurt
- 4 tbsp granola (shop-bought or use Connor's granola – see page 25)
- 1 tbsp coconut flakes
- 1 tsp chia seeds

1 Peel the bananas and cut into slices, then put three-quarters into a blender. Save the rest to decorate.

2 Add the frozen mixed berries, reserving a few for decoration, then add the yoghurt. Try to use frozen Irish berries, as imported frozen berries need to be blanched for 2 minutes to make them safe in line with Food Safety Authority guidelines.

3 Blitz the fruit mixture to a smooth purée. Using a spatula, put into small serving bowls. These can be frozen for a few hours at this point to firm up, which might be necessary if you have used imported berries that needed to be blanched.

4 To serve, decorate the smoothie bowl with the rest of the banana and berries along with the granola, coconut flakes and chia seeds.

HOMEMADE YOGHURT WITH FRUIT

This is great fun and a brilliant way to show how easy it is to make natural foods. Once made it needs to be kept in a warm, draught-free place – an airing cupboard is prefect or beside the Aga if you have one, or near a nice toasty radiator works well too.

Serves 4

- 1 litre (1¾ pints) milk
- 25g (1oz) skimmed milk powder
- 1 tsp natural yoghurt (it must say probiotic on the label)
- 1 small ripe mango
- ¼ ripe pineapple
- 50g (2oz) large seedless purple grapes
- 1 passion fruit
- 1 tbsp shredded fresh mint leaves

1
Pour the milk into a pan over a low heat. As the milk begins to heat up, whisk in the milk powder and allow to just come up to the boil – it will smell sweet and be frothing at the edges. If you have a cooking thermometer it will read 90°C (194°F).

2
Remove the pan from the heat and leave to stand for 10–15 minutes, until the milk is tepid and you can dip your finger in and leave it there for a few seconds. This will read 40°C (104°F).

3
Stir in the yoghurt, then cover the pan with a double layer of tin foil and wrap it in a clean tea towel (or pour into a thermos flask). Leave in a warm place for 4–5 hours to thicken. Pour into a container, cover and chill overnight.

4
The next day, peel the mango and pineapple and cut into bite-sized pieces. Slice the grapes. Halve the passion fruit and scoop in the pulp, then stir the mint into the fruit. Spoon the yoghurt into bowls and decorate with the fruit.

BLACKBERRY & COCONUT CHIA POTS

This breakfast is good enough to have as dessert. Chia seeds are a superfood that have no taste, so they take on the flavour of whatever you mix them with. They need to be left overnight so that they can expand in the liquid you've added to almost triple their size and almost look like frog spawn!

Serves 4

- 225g (8oz) blackberries, plus 6 extra for decoration
- 1 tbsp apple syrup or honey
- 300ml (½ pint) milk (or you could use almond, hazelnut or oat milk if you prefer)
- 1 x 160ml (5½fl oz) tin of coconut milk (Thai Gold)
- 1 tsp vanilla extract
- 6 tbsp chia seeds
- 25g (1oz) coconut flakes

1

Using a fork, mash the blackberries in a large bowl with the apple syrup or honey.

2

Stir in the milk, coconut milk and vanilla.

3

Stir in the chia seeds, then pour into glass pots, leaving plenty of room for expansion. Cover with clingfilm and chill overnight or for at least 6 hours.

4

Remove the clingfilm and cut the blackberries that you saved for decoration in half. Arrange on top of the chia pots with the coconut flakes to serve.

HAZELNUT YOGHURT BROWN BREAD

This is a lovely recipe that we often make at my cookery school. The hazelnut yoghurt gives a sweet nutty flavour, but you could use any natural yoghurt with no added sugar or even a sheep milk yoghurt such as Velvet Cloud instead.

Makes 1 x 900g (2lb) loaf

- 225g (8oz) self-raising flour
- 1 tsp baking powder
- 1 tsp bicarbonate of soda
- 1 tsp salt
- 225g (8oz) wholemeal flour
- 1 egg
- 250g (9oz) hazelnut yoghurt
- 225ml (8fl oz) milk
- ½ tsp rapeseed oil
- 1 tbsp porridge oats
- butter, to serve

1
Preheat the oven to 190°C (375°F/ gas mark 5). Sieve the self-raising flour into a large bowl with the baking powder, bicarbonate of soda and salt, then stir in the wholemeal flour.

2
Mix together the egg, yoghurt and milk in a jug.

3
Slowly add the wet ingredients to the dry and mix well to combine. Be careful not to over mix.

4
Oil a 900g (2lb) loaf tin and add the mixture, then sprinkle over the oats. Bake for 15 minutes, then reduce the temperature to 180°C (350°F/ gas mark 4) and cook for a further 38–40 minutes, until the bread is well risen and cooked through. Serve cut into slices with butter.

ENERGY BREAKFAST BARS

These bars are nutty and filling with the perfect amount of sweetness. Once made they don't need to be baked – only the nuts and seeds are toasted. They also happen to be gluten free and can be vegan if you don't use honey.

Makes 12 bars

- 150g (5oz) whole almonds (skin on)
- 75g (3oz) cashew nuts
- 75g (3oz) sunflower seeds
- 75g (3oz) pumpkin seeds
- 35g (1¼oz) chia seeds
- 35g (1¼ oz) puffed quinoa
- 75g (3oz) dried cranberries
- 150ml (¼ pint) apple syrup or honey
- 3 tbsp rapeseed oil
- 1 tsp fine sea salt
- 2 tsp vanilla extract

1

Preheat the oven to 190°C (375°F/gas mark 5). Toast the almonds and cashews in a 20cm x 12.5cm (8in x 5in) baking tin for 5 minutes. Remove from the oven and add the sunflower, pumpkin and chia seeds and cook 5 minutes, until golden brown. Cool.

2

Tip the cooled toasted nuts and seeds into a large bowl and stir in the puffed quinoa and dried cranberries. Line the baking tin with non-stick baking paper.

3

Bring the syrup or honey, oil, salt and vanilla to the boil in a pan. Reduce the heat and simmer for 10 minutes, stirring occasionally, until it's a deep golden brown. Pour over the nuts and seeds, stirring so everything gets evenly coated.

4

Transfer into the lined baking tin and spread out with a spatula. Leave to cool and harden for 1 hour, then cut into 12 slices. Store in a Kilner jar for three days or freeze and thaw out as needed.

APPLE CRUMBLE MUFFINS

If you don't have paper cases, simply cut small squares of non-stick baking paper and shape into the muffin tins for a stylish result. These are such a treat for a weekend brunch and freeze well, although it's honestly difficult not to eat them all in one go!

Makes 12

- 25g (1oz) plain flour
- ¼ tsp ground cinnamon
- pinch of fine sea salt
- 15g (½oz) chilled butter, diced
- 4 tsp light brown sugar
- 275g (10oz) self-raising flour
- 1 tsp bicarbonate of soda
- 50g (2oz) coconut sugar (or use ordinary caster sugar)
- 2 Irish eating apples, such as Elstar, peeled, cored and chopped
- 120ml (4fl oz) sunflower oil
- 3 tbsp apple syrup or honey
- 2 eggs
- 175ml (6fl oz) buttermilk

1

Preheat the oven to 180°C (350°F/gas mark 4). Line a muffin tin with paper cases. To make the crumble topping, put the plain flour in a bowl with the cinnamon and salt. Rub in the butter until it looks like breadcrumbs, then stir in the brown sugar.

2

To make the muffins, place the self-raising flour, bicarbonate of soda and coconut or caster sugar into a bowl with the apples and mix to combine.

3

Add the oil, apple syrup or honey, eggs and buttermilk to the flour mixture and mix it together, using as few stirs as possible. Using a large spoon, divide the mixture between the muffin cases.

4

Sprinkle an even layer of the crumble topping over each muffin and bake for 18–20 minutes, until the muffins are cooked through. To check, insert a skewer into the centre of a muffin – it should come out clean. Serve warm or cold.

CHOCOLATE CROISSANTS

These bite-sized croissants are surprisingly easy to make and taste so much nicer than the ones you buy in the shops. Little fingers are particularly good for getting the shape correct and you'll have them in the oven in less than 10 minutes.

Makes 12

- 1 x 50g (2oz) bar of milk or plain chocolate
- 1 x 375g (13oz) packet of ready-rolled puff pastry (thawed if frozen)
- 1 egg
- 2 tbsp water
- pinch of fine sea salt

1

Preheat the oven to 220°C (425°F/gas mark 7). Cut the chocolate squares in half. Unroll the puff pastry and cut it into six even-sized squares, then into 12 triangles. Arrange with the points facing you and the widest part away from you.

2

Stretch the tip of each triangle, then place the pieces of chocolate about 2cm (¾in) up from the wide end. Carefully roll up to enclose the chocolate.

3

Gently seal each one with your fingertips and shape it into a crescent. Repeat to make 12 in total.

4

Place the chocolate croissants on a baking sheet lined with non-stick baking paper. Beat the egg, water and pinch of salt and brush this over the croissants. Bake for 10–12 minutes, until puffed up and golden brown.

SPOTTED DOG

This rich traditional white soda bread has dried fruit added so that it looks 'spotted'. In some parts of Ireland it's known as railway cake, as people took it on trains as a snack for their journey.

Makes 1 loaf

- 450g (1lb) plain flour, plus extra for dusting
- 1 tsp bicarbonate of soda
- 1 tsp fine sea salt
- 100g (4oz) sultanas, raisins or currants (or use a mixture)
- 1 tbsp caster sugar
- 1 egg
- 400ml (14fl oz) buttermilk
- butter and strawberry jam, to serve

1
Preheat the oven to 220°C (425°F/gas mark 7). Sift the flour, bicarbonate of soda and salt into a bowl, then stir in the dried fruit and sugar. Beat the egg and buttermilk in a jug. Make a well and pour in most of it (leave about 3 tablespoons).

2
Mix gently to a soft dough, adding more buttermilk as necessary. Knead gently on a lightly floured work surface and shape into a 15cm (6in) round. Place on a baking sheet and cut a cross in the top to let the fairies out! Bake for 15 minutes.

3
Reduce the oven temperature to 200°C (400°F/ gas mark 6) and bake the loaf for another 20–25 minutes, until it's evenly golden and crusty. It should sound hollow when tapped on the bottom. If it doesn't, return it to the oven for another 5 minutes.

4
Transfer to a wire rack and leave to cool for 20 minutes. This is best eaten while it's still warm, as it doesn't store well. Cut into slices at the table with a butter dish and pot of jam so that everyone can help themselves.

LUNCH

CHICKEN NOODLE SOUP

Those indulging in this soup might appreciate bibs! Here I'm serving it with one of my favourite condiments, White Mausu peanut rayu, which is available from most good supermarkets and is made in Dublin. It can jazz up anything, but a drizzle of any chilli sauce also does the trick.

Serves 4

- 1 tbsp rapeseed oil
- 1 small onion, finely chopped
- 1 celery stick, thinly sliced
- 2 garlic cloves, thinly sliced
- 1.2 litres (2 pints) chicken stock (made from cubes is fine)
- 100g (4oz) spaghetti
- 225g (8oz) boneless, skinless chicken fillets, cut into 1cm (½in) strips
- 2 heads of baby pak choi (or use 1 regular size), thinly sliced
- small handful fresh coriander leaves
- about 1 tsp soy sauce
- 1 tbsp White Mausu peanut rayu or chilli sauce (optional)

1
Heat the oil in a large pan over a medium to high heat. Add the onion, celery and garlic and sauté for 4–5 minutes, until softened but not coloured.

2
Pour in the stock and bring to the boil. Break the spaghetti into smaller pieces – halves or quarters of its original size. Add to the pan and simmer for 5 minutes.

3
Add the chicken strips to the pan, then reduce the heat to low and simmer for another 4–5 minutes, until tender and cooked through.

4
Add the pak choi to the pan. Simmer for 1 minute, then ladle into bowls and scatter over the coriander leaves. Season with the soy sauce and serve the peanut rayu or chilli sauce for drizzling on top, if liked.

MEDITERRANEAN PASTA SOUP

Once the pasta is tender, leave this soup to stand for 10 minutes. The cavolo nero will wilt, the pasta swells in the soup and everything just gets better!

Serves 4

- 1 tbsp rapeseed oil
- 1 onion, chopped
- 2 carrots, chopped
- 2 celery stalks, chopped
- 1 tsp fresh thyme leaves
- 1 tbsp tomato purée
- 1 x 400g (14oz) tin of cherry tomatoes
- 450ml (¾ pint) vegetable stock (from a cube is fine)
- 100g (4oz) orzo or any other soup pasta shape
- 100g (4oz) cavolo nero leaves (Tuscan kale or use regular kale)
- sea salt and freshly ground black pepper

1

Heat the oil in a large pan over a medium heat. Add the onion, carrots, celery and thyme and sauté for 6–8 minutes, until the vegetables have taken on a bit of colour.

2

Stir in the tomato purée, then pour in the cherry tomatoes and stock. Bring to the boil over a high heat, stirring.

3

Add the orzo or soup pasta to the pan. Reduce the heat and simmer for 8 minutes, until the pasta is just tender.

4

Remove the tough stalks from the cavolo nero or kale, then roughly tear the leaves into pieces. Add to the pan, season and switch off the heat. Leave the soup to stand for 10 minutes, until the kale is wilted, then ladle into bowls to serve.

CARROT & THYME SOUP

To make this soup, use the freshest carrots you can find. There is no need to peel them so that you get all their goodness. I like to serve it velvety smooth with a lovely swirl of yoghurt to lighten the flavour.

Serves 4

- 25g (1oz) butter
- 1 onion, finely chopped
- 300g (11oz) carrots, scrubbed well and grated
- 1 tsp honey
- ½ tsp apple cider vinegar
- ½ tsp fresh thyme leaves
- 450ml (¾ pint) vegetable stock
- 2 tbsp pumpkin seeds
- 1 tbsp pine nuts
- 2 tbsp thick Greek-style yoghurt
- sea salt and freshly ground black pepper

1
Melt the butter in a large pan over a low heat. Add the onion and sweat for 10 minutes, stirring occasionally.

2
Add the grated carrots to the pan with the honey, vinegar and thyme. Season with salt and pepper and stir well to combine.

3
Pour in the stock, increase the heat to high and bring to the boil. Reduce the heat to a simmer and cook for 10–15 minutes, until the carrots are completely soft. Using a hand-held blender, blitz until smooth.

4
Heat a small frying pan. Add the pumpkin seeds and pine nuts and toast for 2–3 minutes, tossing constantly. Ladle the soup into bowls and add a swirl of yoghurt to each one, then sprinkle over the seeds and nuts.

HAM, CHEESE & TOMATO TOASTIE

There are times when you're starving and need something hot and tasty on the table in less than 10 minutes. Well, this is my go-to recipe and a firm favourite in the Maguire house! You can use a George Foreman grill if you have one, but a good griddle pan works even better in my opinion.

Serves 2

- 25g (1oz) butter, at room temperature
- 4 slices of sourdough bread (or similar), pre-sliced if possible
- 50g (2oz) thinly sliced cooked ham
- 75g (3oz) mature Cheddar cheese, grated
- 2 tomatoes, sliced
- 2 tsp mayonnaise
- 1 tsp English or Dijon mustard (optional)
- sea salt and freshly ground black pepper
- good handful of fresh watercress, to serve

1

Preheat a griddle pan over a medium to high heat. Spread one side of each slice of bread with the butter. Place two pieces of bread in the pan, butter side down, and put a layer of ham on top.

2

Scatter the grated cheese over the ham, then arrange the tomato slices on top. Season with salt and pepper.

3

Spread the unbuttered side of the remaining two slices of bread with the mayonnaise and smear with the mustard, if liked. Use to cover the layered-up slices of bread.

4

Cook the sandwiches for 2–3 minutes on each side, until golden brown. Reduce the temperature if you think that they are browning too quickly. Cut in half and arrange on plates with the watercress to serve.

HAM & COURGETTE QUICHE

This is a quick recipe for a quiche since there's no extra cooking of the filling ingredients. You can alter the flavours depending on what you have in the fridge.

Serves 4

- 200g (7oz) plain flour, plus extra for dusting
- 100g (4oz) cold butter, diced
- 5 eggs
- 1 courgette, peeled into thin ribbons with a peeler
- 50g (2oz) cooked ham chunks
- 50g (2oz) mature Cheddar cheese, finely grated
- 5 tbsp red onion relish (from a jar)
- 250ml (9fl oz) cream
- sea salt and freshly ground black pepper
- green salad, to serve

1
Blitz the flour, butter and 1 teaspoon of salt in a food processor until it looks like breadcrumbs. Beat one of the eggs, then add and pulse until it comes together. Shape into a ball, wrap in clingfilm and chill for 30 minutes.

2
Preheat the oven to 180°C (350°F/ gas mark 4). Roll out the pastry on a floured surface to line a 20cm (8in) loose-bottomed tart tin that's 4cm (1½in) deep. Use the rolling pin to lift it into the tin. Push the pastry into the corners with your thumb.

3
Line the pastry with non-stick baking paper and ceramic baking beans. Bake for 15 minutes, until lightly golden. Remove the paper and beans. Add the courgette ribbons to the pastry with the ham, Cheddar and relish.

4
Whisk the remaining four eggs and cream in a bowl, season to taste and pour it over the filling. Place the quiche on a baking sheet and bake for 40 minutes, until almost set and golden. Rest for 10 minutes, then cut into slices to serve with salad.

CHEESY CHORIZO QUESADILLAS

As soon as we had these, they became a family favourite straight away. Try to buy an uncooked chorizo sausage that feels firm and dry so that the cubes crisp up and pack a powerful flavour punch.

Serves 2

- 1 ripe avocado, halved and stoned
- 1 lime
- 100g (4oz) uncooked chorizo
- 1½ tbsp rapeseed oil
- 2 eggs
- 4 large soft flour tortillas
- 100g (4oz) grated Cheddar and mozzarella cheese mix
- 100g (4oz) small vine tomatoes, sliced
- sea salt and freshly ground black pepper

1

Peel the skin off the avocado and cut into small pieces. Squeeze over the juice from half the lime – cut the other half into wedges to use as a garnish.

2

Cut the chorizo in half and peel off the skin, then chop into small pieces. Heat ½ tablespoon of oil in a large non-stick frying pan over a medium heat. Add the chorizo and cook for 2–3 minutes, until lightly golden. Drain on kitchen paper.

3

Add ½ tablespoon of oil to the pan. Whisk the eggs and season, then add half of the mixture to the pan and stir until it just starts to set. Top with a tortilla and cook for 20 seconds, then flip over and add half the chorizo, cheese and tomatoes.

4

Cover with another tortilla and cook for 1 minute. Slide onto a plate and flip back into the pan. Cook for 1–2 minutes, until golden. Slide onto the work surface and repeat. Cut up and serve on plates with the avocado and lime wedges.

SAVAGE SAUSAGE ROLLS

I've been using the same sausage roll recipe for years, so I had to spend a bit of the time in the kitchen playing around with different ideas. These are particularly good with a dollop of tomato and chilli relish inside.

Serves 4

- 500g (1lb 2oz) sausage meat
- 1 small onion, finely chopped
- 50g (2oz) mature Cheddar cheese, finely grated
- 3 tbsp chopped fresh flat-leaf parsley
- 1 egg
- 500g (1lb 2oz) puff pastry, thawed if frozen
- a little plain flour, for dusting
- 4 tbsp tomato and chilli relish, plus extra to serve
- sea salt and freshly ground black pepper

1

Preheat the oven to 200°C (400°F/gas mark 6). To make the filling, mix the sausage meat in a bowl with the onion, Cheddar and parsley. Season to taste. Crack the egg into a small bowl and beat with a pinch of salt.

2

Cut the pastry in half and roll out each piece on a lightly floured surface to make a long oblong shape that is 33cm x 23cm (13in x 9in). Cut in half again and spread each piece with 1 tablespoon of the relish on top, leaving the edges clear.

3

Form one-quarter of the filling into a log shape and place on the relish-lined pastry approximately 5mm (¼in) from the edge. Brush the edges with the beaten egg, then fold over to enclose the filling and seal the edges with a fork. Repeat.

4

Trim and cut into bite-sized pieces. Brush with beaten egg and arrange on a baking sheet lined with non-stick baking paper. Bake for 18–20 minutes, until cooked through, swapping the baking sheets halfway through. Serve hot or cold with the relish.

STICKY BEEF SKEWERS

These delicious little skewers will have your taste buds singing! You can marinate them overnight, making them a very quick lunch to prepare. They are also quite delicious served at room temperature from a lunchbox that has separate compartments for each component of the dish.

Serves 2

- 225g (8oz) sirloin steak
- 1 garlic clove
- 1 x 2cm (¾in) piece of fresh root ginger
- 1 tsp garam masala
- 4 mini cucumbers
- 1 tsp sesame seeds, plus extra to garnish
- 2 tsp white wine vinegar
- 2 tsp honey
- 1 tbsp rapeseed oil
- 2 large tortilla wraps
- 2 heaped tbsp thick Greek-style yoghurt
- sea salt and freshly ground black pepper

1

Trim the steak of any fat and cut into thin strips, then place in a bowl. Grate in the garlic and ginger. Stir in the garam masala and season with salt and pepper. Set aside for 10 minutes to marinate.

2

Meanwhile, use a vegetable peeler to pare the cucumbers into ribbons and put in a bowl. Add the sesame seeds, vinegar and half of the honey and season with salt and pepper. Gently fold together to combine.

3

Heat a griddle pan over a high heat. Thread the beef onto 6 x 16cm (6¼in) skewers and brush with the oil. Cook for 5–6 minutes, until just tender, turning once. Transfer to a plate, then brush with the remaining honey. Cover with foil to rest.

4

Add the wraps to the griddle pan for about 30 seconds on each side to warm through. Put on plates and smear the yoghurt on top. Add the skewers to one side and the drained cucumber salad to the other to serve.

CHEAT'S HAM & PINEAPPLE PIZZAS

Opinion is divided on this pizza topping. In these extraordinary times the world has been experiencing, some memes have suggested that if 2020 were a pizza, it would have pineapple on it! However, my good friend Orla's daughter Emily is a huge fan, so I've been convinced of its merits.

Makes 2

- 1 Little Gem lettuce
- 6 cherry tomatoes, halved
- 1 tsp rapeseed oil
- ½ tsp balsamic vinegar
- 2 white wraps
- 4 tbsp passata
- 4 slices of wafer-thin ham, torn into pieces
- 1 x 100g (4oz) ball of mozzarella, well drained and torn into pieces
- 50g (2oz) canned pineapple pieces, well drained
- 3 tbsp freshly grated Parmesan cheese

1

Preheat the oven to 220°C (425°F/gas mark 7). Tear the lettuce into pieces and arrange on plates. Scatter the halved cherry tomatoes on top, then drizzle with the oil and vinegar. Season lightly and set aside.

2

Line a baking sheet with non-stick baking paper and place the wraps on top. Using the back of a spoon, spread over the passata until it's almost all the way to the edges. Season lightly with salt and pepper.

3

Arrange the ham on the pizzas, then scatter the mozzarella on top. Scatter over the pineapple, Parmesan and bake for 6–8 minutes, until the cheese is bubbling and golden.

4

Carefully slide the pizzas onto a chopping board. Using scissors, cut into slices and arrange on plates with the salad to serve.

PEPPER & PESTO PIZZA SCROLLS

These irresistible bread swirls use lots of good-quality ready-made ingredients for their filling. You could substitute a pack of white bread mix for this basic dough recipe, but when you see how easy it is to make these, then why bother?

Makes 8

- 500g (1lb 2oz) strong white flour, plus extra for dusting
- 2 tsp fine sea salt
- 300ml (½ pint) lukewarm water
- 1 tbsp rapeseed oil, plus extra for greasing
- 1 x 7g sachet of fast-action yeast
- 100g (4oz) tomato sauce (I like Dunnes Simply Better Tomato and Sweet Garlic Sauce)
- 100g (4oz) pesto (preferably fresh in a carton)
- 150g (5oz) grated Cheddar and mozzarella cheese mix
- 1 x 275g (10oz) jar of chargrilled mixed peppers, drained

1

Sift the flour and salt into a bowl. Make a well and add the water, oil and yeast. Mix to a dough, then turn out and knead on a floured surface for 10 minutes. Put in an oiled bowl, cover with clingfilm and leave in a warm place to double in size.

2

Knock the dough back and knead briefly. Roll out to a 55cm x 35cm (22in x 14in) rectangle. Spread over the tomato sauce, leaving a border, and smear the pesto on top. Scatter over two-thirds of the cheese with the mixed peppers.

3

Roll up one of the short sides and pinch the seam closed. Cut into 8 slices and put cut side up in a baking tin (20cm x 30cm (8in x 12in)) lined with non-stick baking paper. Cover and prove for 30 minutes. Preheat the oven to 180°C (350°F/ gas mark 5).

4

Uncover the rolls and bake for 20 minutes. Scatter over the rest of the cheese and bake for another 15 minutes, until cooked through and golden brown. Leave for 15 minutes before serving warm or at room temperature.

GREEN RICE WITH EGG CONFETTI

The rice should be cooked and cold before you start, or you could use a pouch of pre-cooked rice. If I have any leftover cooked rice, I often pop it into a bag and put it in the freezer, then I use it straight from frozen for this dish, allowing an extra minute or two.

Serves 2

- 2 eggs
- 1 tsp toasted sesame oil
- 2 tbsp rapeseed oil
- 3 spring onions, finely chopped
- 2 garlic cloves, crushed
- 1 tbsp freshly grated root ginger
- 100g (4oz) broccoli, finely chopped (stem and florets)
- 100g (4oz) frozen edamame beans or peas
- 250g (9oz) cooked brown or white rice
- 2 tbsp soy sauce, plus extra to serve
- sweet chilli sauce, to serve (optional)

1
Place a wok or non-stick frying pan over a high heat. Crack the eggs into a bowl and season with salt and pepper, then add the sesame oil and lightly beat.

2
Add half of the rapeseed oil to the wok or pan and tip in the eggs, moving the mixture from side to side so it coats the bottom. Cook for 1 minute, until the edges are crisp and golden. Slide onto a board and cool, then roll it up and shred.

3
Add the rest of the rapeseed oil to the wok and swirl it up the sides. Add the spring onions, garlic and ginger and stir-fry for 20 seconds, until fragrant. Add the broccoli and stir-fry for another 2 minutes.

4
Add the beans or peas and the rice and stir-fry for 3–4 minutes, until the rice is piping hot and the veg are tender. Sprinkle over the soy sauce and the egg confetti, tossing to combine, then divide between bowls with extra soy or chilli sauce, if liked.

MOZZARELLA MUSHROOM GARLIC TOAST

When we were young we picked field mushrooms early in the morning when the weather conditions were right. Sadly, this is almost a thing of the past what with the fertilizer and chemicals that we now use in our fields. This recipe is based on that memory, but long before I had heard of mozzarella!

Serves 2

- 1 small sourdough or rustic baguette, cut into long slices
- 1–2 tbsp rapeseed oil
- 1 garlic clove, unpeeled
- 250g (9oz) open cup mushrooms
- 25g (1oz) butter
- 100g (4oz) baby spinach leaves
- 100g (4oz) buffalo mozzarella (preferably Toonsbridge)
- sea salt and freshly ground black pepper

1
Preheat a griddle pan over a high heat. Brush the baguette slices with the oil. Place the pieces of bread on the griddle and cook for 2–3 minutes, until golden, turning once. You will have to do this in batches.

2
Once all the toasts are cooked, cut the garlic clove in half, then use to rub on one side of the toast. Arrange the toast on a baking tray and set aside.

3
Preheat the grill to medium. Trim off the mushroom stems and cut the cups into slices. Melt the butter in a large non-stick frying pan over a high heat. Add the mushrooms and season, then toss to coat. Cook for 4–5 minutes, until tender.

4
Scatter over the spinach, tossing until just wilted, then arrange on the garlic toasts. Tear the mozzarella on top and flash under the grill for 1–2 minutes, until melted. Serve at once.

SWEET & SOUR STEAK SANDWICH

This steak sandwich is next-level flavour – you'll be licking your fingers once you've finished! It uses all the steak resting juices to soften the bread, making the whole thing just so much more delicious.

Serves 2

- 1 large onion
- 2 tbsp rapeseed oil
- knob of butter
- 2 tbsp dark brown sugar
- 4 tbsp red wine vinegar
- 200–250g (7–9oz) sirloin steak
- 1 garlic clove, unpeeled and cut in half
- 1 small ciabatta loaf
- 2 tbsp mayonnaise
- 1 tsp English mustard
- 50g (2oz) watercress
- sea salt and freshly ground black pepper

1
Cut the onion into 2cm (¾in) rounds. Put a non-stick frying pan over a medium heat. Add half the oil and the butter, then add the onion. Season and toss into an even layer. Sprinkle over the sugar and sauté for 5 minutes, until lightly caramelised.

2
Pour the vinegar into the onion, stirring to combine. Cover with a lid or baking sheet, then reduce the heat to low and simmer for about 20 minutes, until well caramelised. Add a splash of water if you think it needs it.

3
Heat a griddle pan over a high heat. Season the steak and rub with the garlic and the rest of the oil. Cook for 2–3 minutes on each side for medium (or a little longer if you like your meat well cooked). Transfer to a plate to rest.

4
Cut the ciabatta in half, then in half again to open out. Toast on the griddle. Smear the bottoms with the mayonnaise and mustard, then add the watercress. Carve the steak and pile on top with the caramelised onion. Put on the tops to serve.

BEN'S CHICKEN WRAPS

This is Ben's favourite chicken recipe – he just can't get enough of it. The kefir is the magic ingredient, as it tenderises the chicken and helps to impart all the flavours from the spices. I love Blakes Always Organic Natural Kefir from Drumshanbo, which is widely available.

Serves 4

- 2 boneless, skinless chicken fillets, cut into strips
- 1 tsp ground cumin
- 1 tsp sweet paprika
- 1 tsp garam masala
- ½ tsp ground coriander
- 3 tbsp kefir or natural yoghurt
- 1 tbsp rapeseed oil
- 12 radishes
- ¼ cucumber
- 4 large tortilla wraps
- 2 tbsp mayonnaise
- 100g (4oz) butterhead lettuce leaves
- sea salt and freshly ground black pepper

1

Place the chicken strips in a bowl with the cumin, paprika, garam masala, coriander, kefir or yoghurt and oil. Season and stir to combine. Cover with clingfilm and set aside for at least 15 minutes or up to two days in the fridge to marinate.

2

When ready to cook, preheat the oven to 180°C (350°F/ gas mark 4). Line a baking sheet with non-stick baking paper. Using a tongs, arrange the chicken on it. Roast for 6–8 minutes, until cooked through and just beginning to catch around the edges.

3

Trim the radishes and cut into thin slices. Cut the cucumber in quarters, then remove the seeds and cut into dice.

4

Heat a griddle pan until smoking hot. Add the tortillas and cook for about 30 seconds on each side, until lightly charred. Arrange on plates and smear with the mayonnaise, then tear over the lettuce. Add the chicken, radishes and cucumber to serve.

CHICKEN TORTILLA PIES

These are delicious little pockets of goodness that look like a pie but with no pastry involved! Use leftover roast chicken or a rotisserie one straight from the supermarket. These are perfect cold for lunchboxes the next day too.

Serves 4

- 1 small butternut squash
- 1 tbsp rapeseed oil
- 250g (9oz) cooked chicken, shredded into small pieces
- 100g (4oz) frozen petit pois
- 10g (½oz) fresh chives
- 8 tortilla wraps
- 1 egg
- 1 tbsp sesame seeds
- 4 tbsp tomato relish
- sea salt and freshly ground black pepper

1

Preheat the oven to 200°C (400°F/gas mark 6). Cut the top and bottom off the butternut squash, then use a vegetable peeler to pare off the skin. Cut in half, then use a teaspoon to scoop out the seeds. Cut the flesh into 1cm (½in) pieces.

2

Arrange in a baking tin lined with non-stick baking paper and drizzle over the oil, season and roast for 20 minutes, until tender. Cool. Transfer to a bowl and add the chicken and petit pois. Using a scissors, snip in the chives and mix to combine.

3

Put the tortillas on a work surface and spoon 100g (4oz) of the filling onto one half of each tortilla, leaving a 1cm (½in) border. Beat the egg with a pinch of salt, then brush on the border and fold over to enclose, pinching the edges to seal.

4

Arrange the pies on baking sheets lined with non-stick baking paper and brush with the rest of the egg. Sprinkle over the sesame seeds and bake for 10–12 minutes, swapping the baking sheets halfway through. Serve with the tomato relish.

CHICKEN TENDERS & CHILLI COOLER

This buttermilk brine is adapted from the most popular recipe I've ever done for a turkey crown, but the principle is the same. The spiced kefir or buttermilk makes the flesh of the chicken melt-in-the-mouth tender. This could also be served in lettuce cups.

Serves 4

- 300g (11oz) boneless, skinless chicken fillets, cut into strips
- 300ml (½ pint) kefir or buttermilk
- 1 tsp spicy pepper mix or Cajun seasoning
- 50g (2oz) self-raising flour
- 2 eggs
- 100g (4oz) panko breadcrumbs
- 1 tsp rapeseed oil spray
- 6 tbsp thick Greek-style yoghurt
- 1 tbsp mayonnaise
- 1 lime, cut into wedges
- 1 tbsp sweet chilli sauce
- 1 butterhead lettuce
- sea salt and freshly ground black pepper

1

Put the chicken strips in a bowl. Pour in the kefir or buttermilk and add 1 teaspoon of salt with the spicy pepper mix or Cajun seasoning. Stir well, then cover with clingfilm and set aside for 30 minutes or up to two days in the fridge.

2

When you're ready to cook, put the flour on a plate and season with salt and pepper. Crack the eggs into a bowl and season, then whisk lightly. Put the breadcrumbs in another dish.

3

Preheat the oven to 180°C (350°F/gas mark 4). Drain the chicken, then toss in the flour, dip in the egg and coat in the breadcrumbs. Put on a non-stick baking sheet and spray with the oil. Cook for 10–15 minutes, until golden brown.

4

Mix the yoghurt and mayonnaise with a squeeze of lime. Arrange the chicken tenders on plates with the yoghurt mix, then swirl in the sweet chilli sauce. Cut the lettuce into wedges or break into leaves. Add lime wedges to serve.

CHICKEN SATAY WINGLETS

Chicken winglets are the wings that have been sliced through the joint so that you have two meaty pieces and the wing tips are discarded. Most supermarkets sell them like this or just ask your friendly craft butcher to do it for you – they'll be happy to oblige!

Serves 4

- 2 tbsp soy sauce
- 2 tbsp sweet chilli sauce
- juice of 1 lime
- 2 tsp garam masala
- 500g (1lb 2oz) chicken winglets
- 1 x 160ml (5½fl oz) tin of coconut milk (Thai Gold)
- 3 tbsp crunchy peanut butter
- 4 celery sticks (leaves intact)
- 1 bunch of radishes

1

Mix together the soy, chilli sauce and lime juice in a small pan. Pour half into a shallow dish and stir in the garam masala. Add the winglets and mix until evenly coated. Set aside for 1 hour or cover with clingfilm and chill for up to two days.

2

Add the coconut milk and peanut butter to the rest of the soy mixture in the pan. Place over a low heat and simmer for 5 minutes, whisking until smooth. Leave to cool, then stir well and pour into two serving bowls. Cover with clingfilm.

3

Preheat the oven to 220°C (425°F/ gas mark 7). Put the winglets on a baking sheet lined with non-stick baking paper and cook for 20 minutes. Reduce the temperature to 180°C (350°F/gas mark 4) and cook for 25 minutes, until tender and lightly charred.

4

Meanwhile, trim the celery and cut it into small sticks, keeping on any leaves, and trim and slice the radishes. Arrange the celery on a platter with the winglets, bowls of peanut sauce and radishes to serve.

LAMB & CHICKPEA SAMOSAS

Roasting mince of any type before you add it to a dish is a game changer, particularly for these tasty triangles. They will also freeze brilliantly and can be baked to order, making them the perfect portable snack for a lunchbox.

Serves 4

- 225g (8oz) lean lamb mince
- 1 x 400g (14oz) tin of chickpeas, drained and rinsed
- 100g (4oz) frozen peas
- 1 tsp ground cumin
- 1 tsp garam masala
- 1 garlic clove
- 1 x 2cm (½in) piece of fresh root ginger
- handful of fresh mint leaves
- 1 x 275g (10oz) packet of filo pastry, thawed if frozen (6 sheets)
- 75g (3oz) butter, melted and cooled
- 200g (7oz) thick Greek-style yoghurt
- 3 tbsp mango chutney
- salt and freshly ground black pepper

1
Preheat the oven to 190°C (375°F/gas mark 5). Spread the mince out on a baking sheet lined with non-stick baking paper and pat it dry with kitchen paper. Season and roast for 30 minutes, until crisp and golden brown, stirring once or twice.

2
Drain the cooked mince on kitchen paper, then put it in a bowl. Add the chickpeas, frozen peas, cumin and garam masala. Grate in the garlic and ginger and mix to combine, then tear in most of the mint.

3
Unroll the filo, then cut the sheets in half. Brush the top layer with melted butter, then put a heaped spoonful of the filling at the end closest to you and fold it over to enclose. Continue folding until you have a triangle. Repeat.

4
Put on a baking sheet lined with non-stick baking paper. Brush with the rest of the butter. Bake for 15–20 minutes, until golden brown. Put the yoghurt in a bowl and swirl in the chutney and remaining mint. Serve with the samosas.

HAWAIIAN TUNA POKE BOWL

Children are often so much more visual than adults and can decide if they are going to like something at one glance, which can be frustrating. Hopefully this recipe will inspire, plus it's quick to make and great for a lunchbox. It uses a can of tuna instead of fresh, but the flavours really work!

Serves 2

- 250g (9oz) cooked brown rice (leftover or from a pouch)
- 2 tbsp soy sauce
- 1 tbsp rice wine vinegar
- 2 tsp toasted sesame oil
- ½ tsp caster sugar
- pinch of chilli flakes (optional)
- 1 ripe avocado
- ¼ cucumber
- 1 sheet of nori seaweed
- 200g (7oz) tuna in olive oil, drained (Shines, an Irish brand, is my favourite)
- 75g (3oz) frozen edamame beans, thawed
- handful of fresh coriander leaves

1 If using a pouch of rice, cook it in the microwave according to the packet instructions. Leave to cool a little. Fluff up the rice into separate grains and divide between two bowls.

2 To make the dressing, pour the soy sauce into a small bowl and add the rice wine vinegar, sesame oil, sugar and chilli flakes (if using). Whisk or stir to combine.

3 Cut the avocado in half and remove the stone, then peel and slice the flesh. Cut the cucumber into quarters and remove the seeds, then cut into matchsticks. Finely shed the nori seaweed.

4 Arrange the tuna, avocado, cucumber and edamame beans in small piles on the rice and drizzle over the dressing. Scatter over the coriander leaves and nori seaweed to serve.

SALMON & PESTO RAINBOW SALAD

Eat the rainbow with this healthy salad. You'll need a spiralizer, which can be bought online quite cheaply, or you can use a vegetable peeler or julienne grater. Just make sure everything is spanking fresh so that the flavours sing – a farmers market would be a great place to do the shop.

Serves 2

- 10g (½oz) fresh flat-leaf parsley
- 6 tbsp rapeseed oil
- 1 lemon
- 2 large carrots
- 1 beetroot
- 1 large courgette
- large jug of iced water
- 200g (7oz) cooked salmon fillet (shop-bought or leftover)
- 50g (2oz) honey-roasted cashew nuts, roughly chopped
- sea salt and freshly ground black pepper

1
To make the parsley pesto, pick the leaves from the parsley and place in a blender with the oil. Grate in the zest of half the lemon and season lightly, then blitz briefly to a coarse purée. Cut the lemon into cheeks and reserve for garnish.

2
Peel the carrots and beetroot, then using a spiralizer, cut the carrots into long, thin spirals. Repeat with the beetroot and courgette. Put each one into a separate bowl of iced water, as this will help the vegetables to crisp up nicely.

3
Drain the vegetables well and quickly pat dry on kitchen paper. Divide between bowls and flake the cooked salmon on top, discarding any skin and stray bones. Drizzle over the parsley pesto.

4
Scatter the honey-roasted cashews on top of the salads and add a lemon cheek to serve.

DINNER

BEEF & NOODLE STIR-FRY

Striploin steak with the Bord Bia Quality Assured mark is a perfect choice for this stir-fry, but you could use any beef stir-fry strips with good results.

Serves 4

- 200g (7oz) dried wholewheat noodles
- 2 tbsp rapeseed oil
- 4 spring onions, thinly sliced
- 2 garlic cloves, finely grated
- 1 x 2.5cm (1in) piece of fresh root ginger, finely grated
- 300g (11oz) striploin steak, cut into strips
- 1 red pepper, deseeded and thinly sliced
- 100g (4oz) pak choi, sliced
- 1 tbsp soy sauce
- 1 tbsp sweet chilli sauce

1

Place the noodles in a heatproof bowl and cover with boiling water. Set aside for 4 minutes to soften, then drain.

2

Heat a wok or large frying pan until it's very hot. Add the oil and swirl it up the sides. Add the spring onions, garlic and ginger and cook for 20 seconds.

3

Add the beef and stir-fry for 2–3 minutes, until lightly golden. Add the red pepper and pak choi and stir-fry for another 1–2 minutes, until the vegetables are tender but still crunchy.

4

Add the drained noodles, then drizzle in the soy sauce and sweet chilli sauce and toss briefly to combine. Divide between bowls to serve.

EASY SPAGHETTI BOLOGNESE

This clever spag bol can be on the table in not much more than half an hour, but it tastes like it's been simmered for hours. Choose your favourite sauce, but the one that I always use is the Simply Better Italian Tomato and Sweet Garlic Sauce from Dunnes.

Serves 4

- 300g (11oz) lean beef steak mince
- 1 tbsp rapeseed oil
- 1 onion, finely chopped
- 1 celery stalk, finely chopped
- 1 x 375ml (13fl oz) jar of tomato sauce
- 350g (12oz) spaghetti
- 4 tbsp milk
- 50g (2oz) mature Cheddar cheese
- 1 tbsp chopped fresh flat-leaf parsley
- sea salt and freshly ground black pepper

1

Preheat the oven to 190°C (375°F/gas mark 5). Spread the mince out in a baking tin with a wooden spoon and season. Bake for 15 minutes, until it's dark brown and crispy. Drain in a colander.

2

Meanwhile, heat the oil in a frying pan over a medium heat. Add the onion and celery and sauté for 5 minutes, until softened. Stir in the sauce, then fold in the mince. Bring to a simmer and cook for 10 minutes, until the beef is tender.

3

When ready to eat, bring a large pan of salted water to the boil. Swirl in the spaghetti and cook for 8–10 minutes, until tender.

4

Stir the milk into the Bolognese sauce and simmer for another minute or two. Drain the spaghetti and return to the pan, then fold in the sauce until evenly combined. Finely grate over the cheese and scatter over the parsley to serve.

BEEF & CARROT HOT POT

There's nothing like a steaming bowl of stew. Once you've mastered the technique you can swap the meat and vegetables you use. I love one-pot dinners that slowly cook while you're busy with other things. The flavour only improves with time, so keep it covered for up to three days in the fridge.

Serves 4

- 25g (1oz) plain flour
- 300g (11oz) stewing steak pieces
- 2 tbsp rapeseed oil
- 1 large onion, roughly chopped
- 4 carrots, roughly chopped
- 1 tbsp tomato purée
- 600ml (1 pint) beef or chicken stock (from a cube is fine)
- 2 tsp Worcestershire sauce
- 500g (1lb 2oz) baby new potatoes, halved
- 5g (¼oz) fresh flat-leaf parsley
- sea salt and freshly ground black pepper

1

Put the flour in a bowl and season, then add the beef pieces and toss until evenly coated. Heat a flameproof casserole or heavy-based pan over a medium to high heat. Add the oil, then add the beef and quickly sear it on all sides until golden brown.

2

Add the onion and carrots to the casserole, stirring to coat. Sauté for a couple of minutes, scraping the bottom with a wooden spoon.

3

Stir in the tomato purée and cook for 1–2 minutes, then add the stock and Worcestershire sauce. Add the baby potatoes, then reduce the heat, cover and simmer for 1 hour, until meltingly tender but still holding their shape.

4

Strip the leaves from the parsley and roughly chop. Ladle the beef and carrot hot pot into bowls and scatter over the parsley to serve.

MOZZARELLA MEATBALL SUBS

Toonsbridge in Macroom, West Cork makes amazing unpasteurised cow's milk mozzarella that is drier that the more traditional 'fiordilatte' and therefore more suitable for cooking. The milk is supplied to them by Michael Dorney in Kilnaglory and is produced using age-old Neapolitan methods.

Serves 4

- 400g (14oz) lean steak mince
- 300g (11oz) lean pork mince
- 3 tbsp fresh white breadcrumbs
- 1 tbsp milk
- 1 x 250g (9oz) ball of mozzarella (preferably Toonsbridge)
- 1 tbsp rapeseed oil
- 2 x 400g (14oz) tins of finely chopped tomatoes
- 1 tsp caster sugar
- 2 tsp red wine vinegar
- 8 small crusty bread rolls
- 1 head of Little Gem lettuce, shredded
- sea salt and freshly ground black pepper

1

Preheat the oven to 240°C (465°F/ gas mark 9). Heat a flameproof casserole in the oven for 10 minutes.

2

Meanwhile, put the mince, breadcrumbs and milk in a large bowl and season, then mix to combine. Divide into 16 balls. Cut the mozzarella into 16 pieces, then press one into the centre of each meatball to enclose.

3

Carefully remove the casserole from the oven. Add the oil and then the meatballs. Roast for 15–20 minutes, then gently stir in the tomatoes, sugar and vinegar and roast for another 15 minutes, until the meatballs are cooked through.

4

Split open the rolls and smear some of the tomato sauce into each one, then add the shredded lettuce and fill each one with two meatballs. Arrange on plates and put the rest of the sauce on the table for extra dipping.

STIR-FRIED STEAK CHILLI

This super quick dinner is as good as a takeaway and you'll have it on the table in less than 20 minutes. The quality of the tortilla chips can really help to elevate this dish. I normally buy the Blanco Niño tortilla chips that are now available in good supermarkets and are Irish owned.

Serves 4

- 2 tbsp rapeseed oil
- 400g (14oz) stir-fry steak strips
- 1 red onion, thinly sliced
- 1 red pepper, deseeded and thinly sliced
- 1 tbsp Simply Better Spicy Red Pepper and Herb Seasoning or use Cajun seasoning
- 1 mild long red chilli, deseeded and cut into rings (optional)
- 1 x 400g (14oz) tin of finely chopped tomatoes
- 1 x 400g (14oz) tin of black beans, drained and rinsed
- 1 tsp caster sugar
- 1 lime
- handful of fresh coriander leaves
- 1 x 200g (7oz) packet of sea salt tortilla chips
- sea salt and freshly ground black pepper

1

Heat a wok or large non-stick frying pan over a medium to high heat. Add the oil, then tip in the steak and season. Stir-fry for 2–3 minutes, until lightly browned.

2

Add the onion and pepper and stir-fry for another 2–3 minutes, until softened and browning around the edges.

3

Scatter over the spicy red pepper and herb or the Cajun seasoning and the chilli (if using, reserving a little to garnish) and cook for 1 minute. Pour in the tomatoes, beans, sugar and the juice of half the lime. Allow to bubble down for a minute or two.

4

Divide the stir-fried steak chilli between bowls and scatter over the coriander with the rest of the chilli (if using). Serve with tortilla chips and lime wedges to squeeze on top.

MINI SHEPHERD'S PIES

These look super cute and bake perfectly in good-quality muffin tins. If you're worried that they might stick, give the tin a light spray of rapeseed oil and/or line with non-stick baking paper.

Serves 4

- 500g (1lb 2oz) potatoes (such as Rooster), peeled and roughly chopped
- knob of butter
- 50g (2oz) mature Cheddar cheese, grated
- 1 small onion, coarsely grated
- 400g (14oz) lean lamb mince
- 100g (4oz) panko breadcrumbs
- 2 tbsp milk
- 2 tsp tomato purée
- 2 tsp Worcestershire sauce
- 1 egg
- 100g (4oz) extra fine green beans
- sea salt and freshly ground black pepper
- tomato ketchup, to serve

1
Cook the potatoes in a pan of boiling salted water for 20–25 minutes, until tender. Drain and return to the pan to dry out. Mash, then beat in the butter and cheese and season with salt and pepper.

2
Preheat the oven to 180°C (350°F/ gas mark 4). Put the grated onion in a bowl with the mince, breadcrumbs, milk, tomato purée and Worcestershire sauce. Crack in the egg and mix until well combined.

3
Press the mince mixture into eight non-stick muffin tins in a slight dome shape and swirl the cheesy mash on top. Bake in the oven for 20–25 minutes, until golden brown.

4
Meanwhile, cook the green beans in a pan of boiling salted water for 4–5 minutes. Drain and arrange on plates with the shepherd's pies with some tomato ketchup to serve.

CHEESEBURGER SLIDERS

Who doesn't love a burger, and these have plenty of veggies packed inside. Use the best-quality mince you can find with a little bit of fat to keep the burgers nice and succulent. If the weather is fine, put on the tunes and pop them on the barbecue!

Serves 4

- 1 large carrot
- 1 courgette
- 400g (14oz) steak mince (preferably rump)
- 50g (2oz) fresh ciabatta breadcrumbs
- 2 tbsp milk
- 1 tbsp tomato purée
- 75g (3oz) mature Cheddar cheese
- 8 mini burger buns
- 2 tbsp tomato ketchup, plus extra to serve
- 25g (1oz) sliced gherkins, drained (optional)
- sea salt and freshly ground black pepper
- mixed salad, to serve (optional)

1
Trim and grate the carrot and courgette, then squeeze out the excess moisture and put in a bowl. Add the mince, breadcrumbs, milk and tomato purée. Season with salt and pepper and mix well.

2
Divide the mince mix into eight equal potions and flatten into 7.5cm (3in) patties. Preheat a griddle or large non-stick frying pan and cook the burgers for 3–4 minutes on each side.

3
Cut the cheese into slices and arrange on the burgers. Remove from the heat and leave to rest for 5 minutes, giving the cheese time to melt a little.

4
Preheat the grill to medium, then split the buns and lightly toast. Smear the bottoms with ketchup and put the cheesy burgers on top. Add the gherkins (if using), then add the tops. Serve with an extra dish of ketchup and a bowl of salad, if liked.

CHORIZO CHILLI NACHOS

Perfect for a movie night with a bowl of popcorn. These nachos might look like they have a lot of ingredients, but they are actually very easy to make. Have the chilli prepared earlier so that you've everything ready to go – better than any takeaway, I promise!

Serves 4–6

- 100g (4oz) raw chorizo, diced
- 400g (14oz) lean steak mince
- 1 green pepper, deseeded and diced
- 2 mild red chillies, deseeded and thinly sliced (optional)
- 1 tbsp Cajun seasoning
- 4 tbsp tomato purée
- 2 tbsp honey
- 1 tbsp apple cider vinegar
- 1 x 400g (14oz) tin of kidney beans, drained and rinsed
- 1 x 200g (7oz) packet of sea salt tortilla chips (preferably Blanco Niño)
- 100g (4oz) mature Cheddar cheese, grated
- good handful of fresh coriander leaves
- 200g (7oz) soured cream

1
Heat a large non-stick frying pan over a medium heat. Add the chorizo and cook until it starts to sizzle. Add the mince and sauté for 4–5 minutes, until well browned.

2
Add the green pepper, half the chillies (if using) and the Cajun seasoning and sauté for 5 minutes. Stir in the tomato purée, honey, vinegar and beans along with 4 tablespoons of water. Simmer for 15 minutes, stirring, until thickened.

3
Preheat the oven to 180°C (350°F/gas mark 4). Spread the tortilla chips in a foil-lined baking tin and bake for 5 minutes, then spoon over the chilli. Scatter the cheese on top and bake for 6–8 minutes, until bubbling and golden.

4
Scatter the coriander over the nachos with the rest of the chillies (if using). Serve with a bowl of soured cream on the side for dipping.

LAMB SAUSAGE PIZZA BIANCA

There is a strong tradition in Italy of making pizza bianca (white pizza) and this combination is a particularly good one. Press the sage leaves into the toppings so they don't catch and burn.

Serves 4

- 100g (4oz) plain flour, plus extra for dusting
- 75g (3oz) chilled butter, diced
- 100g (4oz) leftover mashed potatoes
- 1 tbsp rapeseed oil, plus extra for drizzling
- 2 small leeks, trimmed and thinly sliced
- 2 lamb sausages (about 300g (11oz))
- 100g (4oz) grated mozzarella cheese
- 100g (4oz) ricotta cheese
- 6 large fresh sage leaves
- 2 tbsp freshly grated Pecorino cheese
- sea salt and freshly ground black pepper
- green salad, to serve

1

Sift the flour into a bowl and season. Rub in the butter to fine breadcrumbs. Quickly stir in the mashed potatoes and mix until you have a soft dough (add 1 tablespoon of iced water if necessary). Wrap in clingfilm and chill for 30 minutes.

2

Preheat the oven to 200°C (400°F/gas mark 6). Heat the oil in a frying pan over a medium heat, then add the leeks and sauté for 5 minutes. Take the sausages out of their casing and shape into small irregular meatballs.

3

Roll out the dough on a lightly floured work surface to a circle about 30cm (12in) in diameter. Using the rolling pin, transfer to a large baking sheet lined with non-stick baking paper. Pinch the edges to make a rim.

4

Sprinkle the mozzarella over the base and place dollops of the ricotta on top. Add the leeks, lamb meatballs and sage. Scatter over the Pecorino and drizzle with oil. Bake for 15–20 minutes, until golden brown. Cut into slices and serve with salad.

BUTTER CHICKEN CURRY

Everyone needs a good curry in their recipe repertoire. You could bulk this up with veg, such as butternut squash or cauliflower, if you like, but this is the basic technique you need to learn, then make it your own!

Serves 4

- 1 onion, roughly chopped
- 4 garlic cloves, roughly chopped
- 1 x 5cm (2in) piece of fresh root ginger, peeled and roughly chopped
- 1 tbsp garam masala
- 200g (7oz) thick Greek-style yoghurt
- 400g (14oz) boneless, skinless chicken cubes (thighs or breasts)
- rapeseed oil, for cooking
- 1 x 400g (14oz) tin of chopped tomatoes
- 1 x 160ml (5½fl oz) tin of coconut cream
- 4 tbsp cashew nut butter
- 225g (8oz) basmati rice
- 450ml (¾ pint) boiling water
- sea salt and freshly ground black pepper

1

Put the onion, garlic and ginger in a food processor with the garam masala, yoghurt and seasoning, then blend to a paste. Mix in a bowl with the chicken, cover with clingfilm and leave for 20 minutes or chill for up to two days.

2

Heat a little oil in a sauté pan over a high heat. Add half of the chicken, reserving the marinade, and sauté for 3–4 minutes, until lightly charred. Repeat and keep on a plate.

3

Reduce the heat to low and return the chicken with the rest of the marinade. Stir in the tomatoes, coconut cream and cashew nut butter and season. Cook for 15 minutes, until the chicken is tender.

4

Rinse the rice in a sieve, then put in a pan with the boiling water and a pinch of salt. Bring to the boil and boil for 1 minute. Cover, reduce the heat to low and simmer for 8 minutes. Leave for 10 minutes. Serve with the butter chicken.

BUTTERMILK SPATCHCOCK CHICKEN

Soaking a spatchcock chicken in buttermilk makes it incredibly tender and juicy. It's actually the easiest way to cook a chicken quickly on the barbecue and should take no more than 45 minutes. It also works in an oven at the same temperature as the potatoes.

Serves 4

- 1 litre (1¾ pints) buttermilk
- 2 tbsp mild curry seasoning
- 2 tsp paprika
- 1 spatchcock chicken
- 4 large baking potatoes
- rapeseed oil, for cooking
- 225g (8oz) tenderstem broccoli
- sea salt and freshly ground black pepper
- lemon aioli, to serve

1
Mix the buttermilk in a large bowl with the curry seasoning, paprika and 2 teaspoons of salt. Add the chicken and make sure it's fully immersed. Cover with clingfilm and leave for 1 hour or up to two days in the fridge.

2
Preheat the oven to 200°C (400°F/gas mark 6). Cut a cross into the top of each potato and bake for 1 hour, until completely tender. Remove and set aside.

3
Heat a gas barbecue to a low heat or wait until the coals are white. Shake the excess marinade off the chicken, then rub with oil. Cook skin side down for 5–10 minutes, until golden, then turn over and cook, covered, for 45 minutes.

4
Rest for 15 minutes, then chop into portions. Cut the potatoes in half, drizzle with oil and season. Toss the broccoli in oil and season. Add to the barbecue and cook for 5–10 minutes, until lightly charred, turning regularly. Serve with aioli.

CHICKEN KORMA SKEWERS

These would also be fantastic cooked on the barbecue. Look for mango chutney in a squeeze bottle, which is perfect for this recipe. If you haven't got almond butter, just use peanut or cashew nut – both will do the trick perfectly!

Serves 4

- 1 x 160ml (5½fl oz) tin of coconut cream
- 2 garlic cloves, finely grated
- 1 x 2.5cm (1in) piece of fresh root ginger, peeled and finely grated
- 2 tbsp crunchy almond butter
- 1 tbsp garam masala
- 500g (1lb 2oz) boneless, skinless chicken (thighs or fillets), cut into 2cm (¾in) pieces
- 4 mini naan breads
- handful of fresh mint leaves
- 6 tbsp thick Greek-style yoghurt
- 2 tbsp mango chutney
- sea salt and freshly ground black pepper

1
Put the coconut cream in a large bowl with the garlic, ginger, almond butter and garam masala and whisk until smooth. Season. Stir the chicken into the marinade. Cover with clingfilm and leave for at least 20 minutes or up to two days in the fridge.

2
Soak 8 x 20cm (8in) bamboo skewers or use metal ones.

3
Preheat the grill to medium. Thread the chicken onto the skewers and arrange in a foil-lined baking tin. Grill for 15 minutes, turning regularly, until tender and lightly charred. Rest for 5 minutes.

4
Place the naan breads under the grill for 5 minutes, turning once. Tear most of the mint into the yoghurt. Serve the skewers and naan on a platter with bowls of the yoghurt and chutney and scatter the rest of the mint on top.

MARMALADE CHICKEN & BROCCOLI

You could change up the vegetables in this tasty stir-fry depending on what you have in the fridge. French beans would work very well, as would sliced mixed coloured peppers, or try sugar snap peas and baby sweetcorn together.

Serves 4

- 350g (12oz) jasmine rice
- 600ml (1 pint) of boiling water
- 400g (14oz) stir-fry chicken strips
- 2 garlic cloves, finely grated
- 1 x 2.5cm (1in) piece of fresh root ginger, peeled and finely grated
- 1 tbsp soy sauce
- 2 tbsp rapeseed oil
- 200g (7oz) tenderstem broccoli
- 175g (6oz) fine cut marmalade
- handful of fresh coriander leaves
- sea salt and freshly ground black pepper

1
Rinse the rice until the water runs clear. Place in a pan with the boiling water and a pinch of salt. Bring to the boil, then cover and reduce the heat to low. Simmer for 15 minutes, until tender. Fluff up with a fork.

2
Meanwhile, put the chicken strips, garlic and ginger into a bowl. Add the soy sauce and stir to combine. Set aside for 20 minutes to marinate if time allows or up to two days in the fridge.

3
Heat a wok or large non-stick frying pan over a medium heat. Add the oil and swirl it up the edges. Add the chicken and stir-fry for 3–4 minutes, until lightly golden.

4
Add the broccoli and sprinkle over 2 tablespoons of water. Steam-fry for 1–2 minutes, then add the marmalade and 2 more tablespoons of water and stir-fry for 2 minutes, until tender and nicely glazed. Serve with the rice and coriander.

MEDITERRANEAN CHICKEN BAKE

Depending on the size of the chicken pieces, this is a generous portion so you could easily get more portions out of it or have some leftover roast chicken for another time – perhaps try my chicken noodle soup (page 46) or chicken tortilla pies (page 74).

Serves 4

- 4 chicken supremes (on the bone)
- 1 tbsp rapeseed oil
- 1 onion, cut into thin wedges
- 3 fresh thyme sprigs
- 500g (1lb 2oz) salad new potatoes, quartered
- 1 small garlic bulb, separated into unpeeled cloves
- 300ml (½ pint) chicken stock (from a cube)
- finely grated rind of 1 lemon
- 200g (7oz) baby plum tomatoes on the vine
- sea salt and freshly ground black pepper

1
Preheat the oven to 180°C (350°F/ gas mark 4). Heat a flameproof casserole over a high heat. Score the chicken skin, then season all over. Add the oil to the casserole, then add the chicken, skin side down. Cook for 2–3 minutes, until browned.

2
Transfer the chicken to a plate. Add the onion and thyme to the casserole and sauté for 2–3 minutes, until golden. Add the potatoes, whole unpeeled garlic cloves and stock, then add the lemon rind and nestle the chicken on top.

3
Cover and bake for 10 minutes, then add the baby plum tomato vines, snipping them into smaller sections with a scissors. Leave the lid off and return to the oven for another 10–15 minutes, until the chicken is cooked through and tender.

4
Arrange the chicken and vegetables on plates. Cut the zested lemon into wedges and use as a garnish to serve.

MAC 'N' CHEESE WITH HAM

This is slightly different than a traditional mac 'n' cheese, which needs a white sauce. It's so delicious and could be bulked up with a bag of baby spinach or some small blanched broccoli florets instead of the salad.

Serves 4

- 225g (8oz) macaroni
- 250g (9oz) mascarpone cheese
- 150ml (¼ pint) milk
- 2 egg yolks
- 1 tsp Dijon mustard
- 175g (6oz) cooked ham pieces
- 100g (4oz) mature Cheddar cheese, grated
- 1 fresh rosemary sprig
- sea salt and freshly ground black pepper
- green salad, to serve (optional)

1
Preheat the oven to 200°C (400°F/gas mark 6). Cook the macaroni in a large pan of boiling salted water for 6 minutes. Drain and set aside.

2
Put the mascarpone in a large bowl and beat in the milk, egg yolks and mustard. Season to taste with salt and pepper, then fold in the cooked macaroni and ham with two-thirds of the cheese.

3
Tip the pasta mixture into a baking dish and scatter over the needles from the sprig of rosemary. Sprinkle the rest of the cheese on top. Bake for 15 minutes, until crisp and golden brown.

4
Serve the mac 'n' cheese straight to the table with a separate bowl of salad, if liked, so that everyone can help themselves.

STICKY PORK RIBS

Slow cook these Asian-style ribs so that they are really tender, then coat in an irresistibly sweet, sticky sauce. Make sure you have plenty of napkins and perhaps some finger bowls of water on hand. They can also be finished on the barbecue if you prefer.

Serves 4

- 2 garlic cloves, grated
- 1 x 2.5cm (1in) piece of fresh root ginger, peeled and grated
- 100g (4oz) light brown sugar
- 4 tbsp hoisin sauce
- 3 tbsp soy sauce
- 3 tbsp rice wine vinegar
- 2 baby back pork ribs (about 1kg (2¼lb))
- 1 tsp toasted sesame seeds
- 5g fresh chives
- 200g (7oz) soured cream
- sea salt and freshly ground black pepper

1

Preheat the oven to 160°C (325°F/ gas mark 3). Put the garlic, ginger, sugar, hoisin, soy and vinegar in a bowl and whisk to combine. Snugly fit the ribs into a roasting tin and pour over 4 tablespoons of the sauce and enough water to just cover.

2

Tightly cover the tin with foil and roast for 2 hours, turning halfway through with a tongs, until the ribs are really tender but not falling apart. Drain off any excess liquid.

3

Increase the oven temperature to 220°C (425°F/ gas mark 7). Arrange the ribs on a foil-lined baking sheet and generously baste with the rest of the sauce. Roast for 25–30 minutes, turning occasionally and basting with the remaining sauce.

4

Cut the racks into individual ribs, then arrange on a platter and scatter over the sesame seeds. Snip the chives into the soured cream in a serving bowl and season. Place the dip alongside with any remaining sauce to serve.

FISH FINGERS & CHIPS

There is a new generation of oil sprays that don't contain lots of extra additives and are a brilliant way of controlling the amount of oil you use. The spritz allows you to give everything a light, even coating of oil so that there is enough to crisp up your food without the need for excess oil.

Serves 4

- 2 large baking potatoes (about 500g (1lb 2oz))
- rapeseed oil, for spraying
- 500g (1lb 2oz) firm white fish fillets, skinned and boned (hake, haddock, pollock or cod)
- 25g (1oz) plain flour
- 2 eggs
- 100g (4oz) panko breadcrumbs
- 1 lemon
- 200g (7oz) thick Greek-style yoghurt
- small handful of fresh flat-leaf parsley leaves
- sea salt and freshly ground black pepper

1
Preheat the oven to 200°C (400°F/gas mark 6). Cut the potatoes into thick chips and spread out in a baking tin lined with non-stick baking paper. Spray lightly with oil and season with salt. Roast for 20 minutes.

2
Cut the fish into 7.5cm (3in) strips, 2.5cm (1in) wide. Season the flour on a plate. Beat the eggs with a pinch of salt. Put the breadcrumbs in a bowl. Toss the fish in the flour, then using a tongs, dip in the egg and toss in the breadcrumbs.

3
Put the fish fingers on a baking sheet lined with non-stick baking paper and spray with oil. Turn the chips over, then put the fish on the top shelf and roast for 10 minutes. Turn over the fish and cook for another 5 minutes, until golden.

4
Cut the lemon into four wedges for garnish, then squeeze the rest into the yoghurt. Season and snip in the parsley with some scissors, stirring to combine. Put the fish and chips on plates with the yoghurt tartare sauce and lemon wedges.

SALMON WITH GREEN COUSCOUS

A quick and easy recipe that looks super impressive and is as nice cold as it is hot. Perfect for a summer evening to eat out in the garden.

Serves 4

- 4 x 100g (4oz) salmon darnes (organic if possible)
- 2 tsp harissa seasoning
- 2 tbsp rapeseed oil
- 300g (11oz) couscous
- 300ml (½ pint) boiling water
- 100g (4oz) baby courgettes
- 100g (4oz) asparagus spears
- 200g (7oz) purple sprouting broccoli
- handful of fresh flat-leaf parsley leaves
- sea salt and freshly ground black pepper

1
Preheat the oven to 190°C (375°F/gas mark 5). Arrange the salmon in a baking tin lined with non-stick baking paper and sprinkle over the harissa seasoning. Season and drizzle with half the oil. Roast for 6–8 minutes, until just tender.

2
Place the couscous in a heatproof bowl. Add the rest of the oil and season with salt. Pour in the boiling water, cover and leave for 5 minutes.

3
Pare the courgettes into ribbons. Trim and cut the asparagus and broccoli in half. Place in a steamer and cook for 2 minutes, until they still have a little crunch, then gently fold into the couscous.

4
Arrange the green vegetable couscous on plates and tear over the parsley. Add a salmon darne to each one to serve.

BUTTERNUT & RICOTTA LASAGNE

If you're going to make a lasagne, you might as well make a big one. This uses the prepared diced butternut squash that is available in all supermarkets, but you could prepare your own – just buy two whole ones instead.

Serves 4–6

- 4 x 300g (11oz) packets of diced butternut squash (or use 1 butternut squash)
- 1 tbsp chopped fresh sage, plus a handful of extra leaves
- 2 tbsp rapeseed oil, plus extra for greasing
- 2 x 250g (9oz) tubs of fresh Italian ricotta cheese
- 100g (4oz) freshly grated Parmesan cheese, plus extra
- 2 eggs
- 5 tbsp milk or cream
- 6 fresh pasta lasagne sheets
- sea salt and freshly ground black pepper
- wild rocket, spinach and cress salad

1

Preheat the oven to 190°C (375°F/gas mark 5). Put the butternut in a roasting tin with the chopped sage and oil. Season and roast for 15–20 minutes, until tender.

2

Mix the ricotta, Parmesan, eggs and milk or cream in a bowl. Season with salt and pepper. Lightly grease a 24cm (9½in) baking dish. Put two lasagne sheets on the bottom and scatter over half of the roasted butternut.

3

Add another layer of lasagne, then spread with half of the ricotta mix and the rest of the butternut. Add the remaining lasagne sheets, then cover with the rest of the ricotta mix. Scatter over a little more Parmesan. Cover with tin foil.

4

Bake for 30 minutes, then uncover and bake for 20–25 minutes, until golden. Sauté the sage in oil in a frying pan over a medium heat until crisp and scatter over the lasagne. Allow to stand for 5 minutes, then serve with the salad.

VEGGIE BOSS BURGERS

These are my favourite veggie burgers and can easily be popped on the barbecue. They're so packed full of goodness and flavour that no one will miss the meat! The ingredient list might look a little long, but the recipe really doesn't take much time to prepare.

Serves 4

- knob of butter
- 1 onion, finely chopped
- 1 large carrot, grated
- 2 courgettes, grated
- 1 x 400g (14oz) tin of chickpeas, drained and rinsed
- 125g (4½oz) fresh ciabatta breadcrumbs
- 1 egg yolk
- 1 tbsp garam masala
- 2 tbsp crunchy nut butter (almond, cashew or peanut)
- rapeseed oil, for brushing
- 4 sourdough or ciabatta buns
- 4 tbsp mayonnaise
- good handful of crisp lettuce leaves
- sea salt and freshly ground black pepper

1
Melt the butter in a non-stick frying pan over a medium heat. Add the onion and sauté for 5 minutes, until golden. Add the carrot and courgettes and sauté for another 5 minutes, until soft. Leave to cool.

2
Place the chickpeas in a large bowl and roughly mash with a potato masher. Add the vegetable mix, then add the breadcrumbs, egg yolk, garam masala and nut butter. Shape into 4 x 10cm (4in) patties. Put on a plate and chill for at least 2 hours.

3
Return the frying pan to a medium-high heat. Brush the burgers with a little oil and cook for 5–6 minutes on each side, turning once.

4
Split the buns and toast under a medium grill. Smear the mayonnaise on the buns, then add a layer of lettuce and a veggie burger to serve.

BAKING & TREATS

CARAMEL SWIRL BROWNIES

~~~~~~~~~~~~~~~~~~~~~~~~~~~~~

These are the most delicious brownies, made all the more decadent with the caramel swirl (which can be left out if you prefer). When lining a cake tin with paper, it's always worth leaving a little extra hanging over the edges so that your bake is easier to pull out once it has cooled.

Makes 16 squares

- 175g (6oz) butter
- 175g (6oz) dark chocolate (55–70% cocoa solids), finely chopped
- 3 eggs
- 225g (8oz) light brown sugar
- 1 tsp vanilla extract
- 75g (3oz) plain flour (or you can use gluten-free)
- 3 tbsp cocoa powder
- 1 x 400g (14oz) can or jar of caramel

1

Preheat the oven to 180°C (350°F/ gas mark 4). Line a 20cm (8in) cake tin with non-stick baking paper. Melt the butter in a pan, then take the pan off the heat and add the chocolate. Leave the chocolate to melt, then stir until smooth.

2

Whisk the eggs, sugar and vanilla extract for 3 minutes. With the whisk still going, pour in the melted chocolate mixture.

3

Sieve the flour and cocoa powder together into a bowl, then fold this into the wet ingredients with a spatula or metal spoon.

4

Spoon into the prepared tin. Add dollops of the caramel all over the surface, then swirl with a toothpick or skewer. Bake for 20–25 minutes, until dry on top but still slightly gooey and fudgy inside. Leave to cool, then cut into squares.

BANANA LOAF WITH PEANUT FROSTING

I think it's safe to say that most households have made banana bread in some form over the last year, which is why I decided to come up with a different take. The bananas in this loaf are first caramelised, elevating the flavour hugely.

Makes 1 large loaf

- 1 tbsp hot water
- 125g (4½oz) light brown sugar
- 100g (4oz) butter
- 3 large bananas, peeled and cut into slices
- 1 egg
- 200g (7oz) plain flour
- 1 tsp baking powder
- ½ tsp fine sea salt
- pinch of bicarbonate of soda
- 150g (5oz) smooth peanut butter, plus 2 tbsp extra for drizzling
- 75g (3oz) icing sugar
- 50g (2oz) unsalted butter, at room temperature
- 2 tbsp cream

1

Put a frying pan over a medium heat. Add the water and 25g (1oz) of the brown sugar. Cook for 2–3 minutes, until golden. Stir in a knob of the butter, add the bananas and cook until golden brown, then mash in a bowl.

2

Preheat the oven to 180°C (350°F/gas mark 4). Melt the rest of the butter in the frying pan, then add to the bananas with the remaining brown sugar and the egg, flour, baking powder, salt and bicarbonate of soda.

3

Mix with a spatula, then use to fill a 1.2 litre (2 pint) loaf tin lined with non-stick baking paper. Bake for 40–45 minutes, until a skewer comes out clean. Cool in the tin for 10 minutes, then transfer to a wire rack and leave to cool completely.

4

To make the frosting, place the peanut butter, icing sugar and unsalted butter in a bowl and beat until light and fluffy. Add the cream and beat again until smooth. Spread over the loaf and drizzle over the extra peanut butter to serve.

MR WHIPPY CUPCAKES

These cupcakes would bring a smile to anyone who is lucky enough to be offered one! I have made them in honour of Mr Whippy, which we love to get as a treat on a trip to the seaside. If you use coconut sugar you'll get a much lighter crumb and you can even reduce the amount to 100g (4oz).

Makes 12

- 150g (5oz) butter, at room temperature
- 150g (5oz) coconut or caster sugar
- 3 eggs
- 150g (5oz) plain flour
- 1½ tsp baking powder
- 350g (12oz) icing sugar
- 150g (5oz) unsalted butter, at room temperature
- 2 tsp vanilla extract
- a few drops of blue and pink food colouring
- 2 tbsp sprinkles
- 12 mini chocolate flakes

1

Preheat the oven to 180°C (350°F/gas mark 4). Using an electric mixer or a wooden spoon, beat the butter and coconut or caster sugar together in a bowl until pale and fluffy.

2

Beat in one of the eggs and half of the flour with the baking powder, then beat in the remaining two eggs and flour until smooth.

3

Divide the mixture between a 12-hole muffin tin lined with paper cases and smooth the tops with the back of a spoon. Bake for 15 minutes, until a skewer comes out clean. Leave to cool.

4

Beat the icing sugar, unsalted butter and vanilla until fluffy. Put into two bowls and add each food colouring separately. Fill two piping bags fitted with fluted nozzles and pipe on the cupcakes in a swirl. Decorate with sprinkles and flakes to serve.

TOFFEE POPCORN CHOCOLATE CAKE

This celebration cake has all the grandeur of a posh shop-bought version at a fraction of the price. It has no icing around the edges, so you can see the layers in all their glory. If you don't fancy the toffee popcorn topping, replace it with your favourite sweets.

Serves up to 20

- 350g (12oz) butter, at room temperature
- 325g (11½oz) light brown sugar
- 275g (10oz) self-raising flour
- 6 large eggs
- 4 tbsp milk
- 2 tsp vanilla extract
- 50g (2oz) cocoa powder
- ½ tsp baking powder
- 250g (9oz) cream cheese
- 125g (4½oz) icing sugar
- 75g (3oz) unsalted butter, at room temperature
- 150g (5oz) toffee popcorn

1

Preheat the oven to 180°C (350°F/gas mark 4). Using an electric mixer or a wooden spoon, beat the butter and brown sugar in a bowl until pale and fluffy.

2

Beat in half of the flour, eggs and milk with all of the vanilla. Using a spatula, gently stir in the rest of the flour, eggs and milk with the cocoa and baking powder until just combined.

3

Divide the mixture between 3 x 20cm (8in) loose-bottomed cake tins lined with non-stick baking paper. Bake for 30 minutes, until a skewer comes out clean. Leave in the oven to cool completely.

4

Mix the cream cheese, icing sugar and unsalted butter to combine. Put a dollop on a cake stand and place the first cake layer on top. Spread with a third of the icing and continue layering, finishing with the icing. Pile the popcorn on top to serve.

BLACKBERRY & RICOTTA TURNOVERS

These pies are perfect for a picnic or to serve as a dessert. Try to make them during blackberry season and pick your own if at all possible.

Makes 6

- 175g (6oz) plain flour, plus extra for dusting
- pinch of fine sea salt
- 75g (3oz) icing sugar
- 75g (3oz) chilled butter, diced
- 2 eggs
- 1 tsp ice-cold water, plus extra for sealing
- 225g (8oz) fresh blackberries
- 50g (2oz) caster sugar
- 150g (5oz) ricotta cheese

1

Sift the flour, salt and 50g (2oz) of the icing sugar into a bowl and rub in the butter until it resembles breadcrumbs. Beat one of the eggs with the water, then add and mix to a dough. Shape into a ball, wrap in clingfilm and chill for 30 minutes.

2

Soften the blackberries in a pan with half the caster sugar. Cool. Beat the remaining egg in a small bowl. Put half into a larger bowl and mix in the ricotta with the rest of the sugar. Stir the remaining 25g (1oz) of icing sugar into the small bowl.

3

Preheat the oven to 180°C (350°F/gas mark 4). Roll out the pastry on a floured work surface and stamp out 6 x 10cm (4in) rounds and 6 x 8cm (3¼in) rounds. Using the smaller rounds, divide the blackberry filling between them, leaving a border.

4

Top with the ricotta mix, then cover with the larger rounds. Brush with water and crimp to seal. Put on a baking sheet lined with non-stick baking paper, brush over the glaze and make a small cross on each one. Bake for 25–30 minutes, until golden. Serve warm or at room temperature.

CHOCOLATE BROWNIE S'MORES

S'mores are an American campfire treat where you melt marshmallows on sticks and sandwich them between shop-bought biscuits and a square of chocolate. The heat from the marshmallows melts the chocolate, so instead I'm using a gooey chocolate brownie cookie.

Makes 12

- 350g (12oz) plain chocolate, finely chopped
- 40g (1½oz) butter
- 2 eggs
- 150g (5oz) caster sugar
- 1 tsp vanilla extract
- 3 tbsp plain flour
- ¼ tsp baking powder
- 12 marshmallows

1

Preheat the oven to 180°C (350°F/gas mark 4). Place 200g (7oz) of the chocolate and the butter in a heatproof bowl. Set over a pan of simmering water, but the water must not touch the bottom of the bowl. Leave to melt, then stir until smooth. Cool.

2

Break the eggs into a large bowl and whisk until doubled in size, then whisk in the sugar and vanilla until you have a stiff mixture that can hold a trail of the figure eight. Sift over the flour and baking powder and gently fold in.

3

Add the melted chocolate with the rest of the chopped chocolate and fold in gently. Leave to stand for 10 minutes, then spoon tablespoons onto baking sheets lined with non-stick baking paper – you need 24 in total. Bake for 8 minutes. Cool.

4

Thread the marshmallows onto metal skewers. Hold the skewers over a campfire or barbecue (or you could use a gas stove or hearth fire), turning slowly until toasted. Use to sandwich together the chocolate brownie cookies to serve.

OREO COOKIES & CREAM PIE

This is really a cheesecake and is possibly the most decadent one you'll ever taste. A little will go a long way and it will keep brilliantly in the fridge for up to three days. You can use any chocolate cream-filled biscuit, but Oreos are hard to beat!

Serves 8–10

- 3 x 150g (5oz) packets of Oreo cookies
- 125g (4½oz) butter
- 250g (9oz) cream cheese
- 300ml (½ pint) cream
- 25g (1oz) icing sugar
- 1 tsp vanilla extract
- 2 tsp chocolate sprinkles

1
Place 150g (5oz) of the cookies in a food processor and pulse to coarse breadcrumbs (or put them in a polythene bag and bash with a rolling pin). Melt the butter in a small pan or in the microwave and stir it into the crumbs.

2
Using the back of a spoon, press into a 20cm (8in) loose-bottomed fluted tart tin that is 4cm (1½in) deep. Chill for 30 minutes.

3
Place the cream cheese in a bowl with the cream, sugar and vanilla and whisk to stiff peaks. Spread a layer on the cookie base, then cover with a layer of cookies, pressing down gently. Repeat, finishing with a layer of the cream mix.

4
Chill the pie for at least 2 hours or overnight is perfect. Put the pie on tins so that you can easily remove it from the tin and slide onto a cake stand. Scatter over chocolate sprinkles and cut into slices to serve.

OATY MELTING MOMENTS

This is a version of a recipe that I've been making since I was a boy but I've added some oats here for extra goodness. They are delicious warm out of the oven with a cup of tea or a mug of hot chocolate.

Makes 18

- 225g (8oz) butter, at room temperature
- 125g (4½oz) caster sugar
- 1 egg
- 2 tsp vanilla extract
- 275g (10oz) self-raising flour
- 175g (6oz) porridge oats, plus an extra handful for rolling

1

Preheat the oven to 180°C (350°F/ gas mark 4). Beat the butter and sugar in a large bowl until light and fluffy. I use a hand-held electric mixer, but a wooden spoon works too.

2

Add the egg and vanilla to the butter mix and beat well to combine. Tip in the flour and oats and stir gently until just combined.

3

Place a handful of oats on the work surface. Take a heaped tablespoon of the mix and using your hands, roll into a ball. Gently roll in the oats, then put on a large baking sheet lined with non-stick baking paper, pressing them down lightly.

4

Repeat until you have 18 in total, then bake for 15–20 minutes, until cooked through and golden brown. Leave to cool a little before serving.

SNICKERS SHORTBREAD

This recipe is from Emily Stafford, who developed it for a school cookery competition and has very kindly shared it with me. It makes plenty so it's perfect for a party or bake sale. Any leftovers keep well in an airtight container for up to three days.

Makes about 30 bars

- 175g (6oz) plain flour
- 75g (3oz) semolina
- 75g (3oz) caster sugar
- 275g (10oz) butter, cut into cubes, at room temperature
- 100g (4oz) light brown sugar
- 2 x 400g (14oz) tins of condensed milk
- ½ tsp sea salt flakes
- 150g (5oz) jumbo salted peanuts
- 300g (11oz) milk or dark chocolate, broken into squares

1

Preheat the oven to 180°C (350°F/gas mark 4). Mix the flour, semolina and caster sugar in a bowl. Rub in 175g (6oz) of the butter to resemble fine crumbs. Press into a 37.5cm x 25.5cm (15in x 10in) baking tin lined with non-stick baking paper.

2

Prick with a fork and bake for 16–18 minutes, until firm and golden. Put the rest of the butter in a heavy-based pan with the light brown sugar and condensed milk and heat gently until the sugar has dissolved. Bring to the boil, stirring.

3

Reduce the heat and simmer gently, stirring, for about 20 minutes, until the mixture has thickened and darkened. Stir in the salt until dissolved. Scatter the peanuts over the shortbread, then pour over the caramel. Cool for 15 minutes.

4

Melt the chocolate in a bowl set over a pan of simmering water. Cool, then pour it over the caramel and spread the top very gently. Cool, then remove from the tin, carefully peel off the baking paper and cut into bars.

COCONUT & STRAWBERRY RICE PUDDING

We probably make this rice pudding more often than any other dessert in our house.
It needs 750ml (1¼ pints) of liquid in total, so use whatever combination you fancy – even semi-skimmed milk works well – then top it with your favourite fresh or stewed fruit.

Serves 4–6

- 1 x 400ml (14floz) tin of coconut milk
- 200ml (7fl oz) milk
- 150ml (¼ pint) cream
- 100g (4oz) short-grain pudding rice
- 25g (1oz) butter
- 1 vanilla pod, split in half lengthways and seeds scraped out
- 125g (4½oz) caster sugar
- 500g (1lb 2oz) strawberries, trimmed
- 2 tbsp lemon juice

1 Place the coconut milk, milk and cream in a pan over a medium heat and bring to a simmer. Stir in the rice, butter and vanilla pod and seeds with 75g (3oz) of the sugar. Stir until the sugar has dissolved.

2 Reduce the heat to the lowest setting and cook for 35–40 minutes, until the rice is tender and creamy. Stir frequently to ensure it does not stick at the bottom.

3 Cut each strawberry in half or quarters and put in a saucepan with the rest of the sugar and the lemon juice. Heat gently until the sugar dissolves, then bring to a simmer. Cover and cook for 3 minutes, until syrupy. Cool.

4 Spoon the coconut rice pudding into bowls and swirl in the strawberry compote to serve.

ROCKY ROAD BITES

This super easy recipe was originally developed as an ice cream flavour by William Dreyer in Oakland, California. The Irish have certainly taken it to their hearts and you'll find a version of it in most cafés. These would also make a lovely present wrapped in tissue paper in a nice box.

Makes about 24 squares

- 8 x 58g (2¼oz) Mars bars, chopped
- 8 tbsp pouring golden syrup
- 225g (8oz) butter
- 2 x 40g (1½oz) Crunchie bars, finely chopped
- 100g (4oz) Rice Krispies
- 100g (4oz) mini marshmallows
- 1 x 200g (7oz) bar of milk chocolate, broken into squares

1

Place the Mars bars in a pan with the golden syrup and 175g (6oz) of the butter. Cook over a low heat for 3–4 minutes, until melted, then beat until smooth. Cool.

2

Fold the Crunchies, Rice Krispies and mini marshmallows into the Mars bar mixture until well combined. Transfer to a 20cm (8in) square tin lined with non-stick baking paper. Spread out evenly with a spatula.

3

Melt the milk chocolate with the rest of the butter in a heatproof bowl set over a pan of simmering water, making sure the water doesn't touch the bottom of the bowl.

4

Spread or drizzle in an even layer over the chocolate mixture and set aside for at least 1 hour, until set firm. Cut into squares and arrange on a cake stand to serve. The squares will keep well for up to a week in the fridge.

OATMEAL CHOCOLATE CHIP COOKIES

These big chewy cookies are best served warm. The trick is to slightly under-bake them so that they are still a little soft and chewy once they have cooled. Use your favourite chocolate chips, or if you want them a little healthier try adding raisins or dried cranberries instead.

Makes 10

- 100g (4oz) butter, at room temperature
- 100g (4oz) light brown sugar
- 1 egg
- 2 tsp vanilla extract
- 125g (4½oz) porridge oats
- 75g (3oz) chocolate chips (dark, milk or white or use a mixture)
- 100g (4oz) self-raising flour
- pinch of sea salt flakes

1
Preheat the oven to 180°C (350°F/gas mark 4). Beat the butter and sugar until light and fluffy. Beat in the egg and vanilla, then stir in the oats, chocolate chips, flour and salt until just combined.

2
Divide the mixture into 10 equal-sized blobs. Put them on two large baking sheets lined with non-stick baking paper, leaving plenty of room between them so they can spread out.

3
Bake in the oven for 10–12 minutes, swapping around the sheets after 5 minutes to ensure they cook evenly.

4
Remove the cookies from the oven and leave them to cool a little before serving.

APRICOT THUMBPRINT COOKIES

These classic cookies are made with a simple dough, rolled in sparkling sugar, then indented and filled with jam. They are definitely one of my all-time favourite cookies and the filling options are absolutely endless.

Makes 12

- 200g (7oz) butter, at room temperature
- 100g (4oz) caster sugar
- 1 egg yolk
- 225g (8oz) plain flour
- 50g (2oz) ground almonds
- pinch of fine sea salt
- 50g (2oz) granulated sugar, for dusting
- 4 tbsp apricot jam

1

Beat the butter and caster sugar in a bowl until light and fluffy. I use a hand-held electric mixer but a wooden spoon also works.

2

Add the egg yolk, flour, ground almonds and salt and gently mix together until just combined. Form into a ball, then wrap in clingfilm and chill for 1 hour to firm up.

3

Preheat the oven to 180°C (350°F/ gas mark 4). Roll the dough into 12 even-sized balls, then roll in the granulated sugar and put on a baking sheet lined with non-stick baking paper. Using your thumb, firmly press down the centre of each one.

4

Fill each cookie with 1 teaspoon of the jam. Bake for 12–14 minutes, until the cookies are firm and lightly golden. Leave to cool before serving.

MINI RASPBERRY PAVLOVAS

If you want these to look really professional, use a mechanical ice cream scoop to measure out the uncooked meringue, then carefully make the indentations with a teaspoon. Once the pavlovas are baked, the cream and fruit will sit in there.

Makes 18

- 4 egg whites, at room temperature
- 225g (8oz) caster sugar
- 1 tsp cornflour
- 1 tsp lemon juice
- 100g (4oz) white chocolate, broken into squares
- 300ml (½ pint) cream
- 50g (2oz) icing sugar
- 500g (1lb 2oz) fresh raspberries
- 2 tbsp toasted flaked almonds

1
Preheat the oven to 140°C (275°F/gas mark 1). Whisk the egg whites in a large clean, dry bowl until soft peaks have formed. Add a quarter of the caster sugar and whisk until stiff.

2
Continue whisking and add the rest of the sugar in a thin steady steam until you have a nice shiny meringue. Using a spatula, fold in the cornflour and lemon juice.

3
Dab blobs of the meringue under the corners of two baking sheets lined with non-stick baking paper. Put 18 even-sized meringues on top, then make an indentation in the centre of each one. Bake for 1–1¼ hours, until firm. Cool.

4
Melt the chocolate in a bowl over a pan of simmering water, then cool. Whisk the cream and icing sugar to soft peaks. Use to fill the pavlovas and decorate with the raspberries, almonds and a drizzle of the chocolate to serve.

MANGO & STRAWBERRY ICE POPS

These are brilliant to stock up your freezer with for the summer and will save you a fortune on ice creams! I love this flavour combination and the slices of strawberries really make the colours pop.

Makes 12

- 5 limes
- 1 x 170g (5¾oz) tin of condensed milk
- 1 x 160ml (5½fl oz) tin of coconut milk (Thai Gold)
- 1 large ripe mango
- 150g (5oz) small strawberries

1

Finely grate 2 teaspoons of the rind from the limes, then give them a good roll before cutting them in half and squeezing the juice. Put the rind in a Pyrex jug, then sieve in the juice. Whisk in the condensed milk and coconut milk and set aside.

2

Peel the mango and cut off the flesh – you need about 200g (7oz). Place in a small blender or NutriBullet with 6 tablespoons of the lime and milk mixture. Blitz to a purée – you need 300ml (½ pint) in total.

3

Cut the stalks off the strawberries and cut into slices, then divide between the ice pop moulds. Alternate pouring the lime and coconut mix and the mango purée into the moulds and swirl gently with a wooden skewer.

4

Put the ice pop sticks into the filled moulds and freeze for at least 4 hours or overnight is best, until set. To serve, quickly dip the ice pop moulds into hot water to loosen the ice pops and hand around immediately.

RASPBERRY RIPPLE MILKSHAKES

Who doesn't love a milkshake? The key ingredients are milk and ice cream, but depending on how healthy you want to be you can use frozen yoghurt or your favourite decadent vanilla ice cream.

Makes 4

- 2 tbsp lemon juice
- 4 tbsp hundreds and thousands sprinkles
- 350g (12oz) frozen raspberries
- 300ml (½ pint) Irish apple juice
- 3 tbsp apple syrup or honey
- 600ml (1 pint) skimmed milk
- 500ml (18fl oz) frozen yoghurt or vanilla ice cream

1
Choose four suitable glasses and dip the rims into a small dish of the lemon juice, then dip into a separate dish of the sprinkles so that the rims are evenly coated. Put into the fridge to chill.

2
Put the raspberries in a blender or NutriBullet with the apple juice and the apple syrup or honey. Blend to a purée, then pass through a sieve into a small jug. Chill.

3
Rinse out the blender, then add the milk and the frozen yoghurt or ice cream. Blitz until smooth.

4
Divide the milkshake between the glasses, being careful of the rims, then drizzle in the raspberry coulis. Swirl with a straw to create a ripple effect. Serve at once with straws.

BANOFFEE ICE CREAM SUNDAES

This is a super easy banana ice cream that uses ready-made custard, so most of the work is done for you. You can use any toffee sauce, but dulce de leche is lovely and thick with a deep caramel colour, as it's made from condensed milk mixed with a proper caramel.

Serves 4

- 6 ripe bananas
- 600ml (1 pint) ready-made chilled custard
- 50g (2oz) pecan nuts
- 6 tbsp dulce de leche or toffee sauce
- 2 crunchy oat biscuits
- 50g (2oz) milk chocolate, finely grated

1

Peel and slice four of the bananas and arrange on a baking sheet lined with non-stick baking paper that will fit into your freezer. Freeze for 1 hour or until frozen.

2

Remove the bananas from the freezer and put into a food processor with the custard. Blitz to blend, then pour into a 1 litre (1¾ pints) plastic container. Put in the freezer with the serving glasses for at least 4 hours or overnight is fine too.

3

Toast the nuts in a frying pan for 4–5 minutes, tossing occasionally. Tip out onto a cutting board and roughly chop. Heat the dulce de leche or toffee sauce in a small pan until it's runny. Peel and thinly slice the remaining two bananas.

4

Remove the glasses from the freezer. Add a layer of the sliced banana and crumble in the biscuits. Top with a couple scoops of the banana ice cream, drizzle over the dulce de leche and scatter over the grated chocolate and pecans to serve.

WARM APPLE PIE

For the best apple pie, use a variety of apples to achieve the wonderful combination of sweet and tart flavours. The various types will also cook differently, with some melting down completely while others will hold their shape.

Serves 6–8

- 300g (11oz) plain flour, plus extra for dusting
- 2 tbsp icing sugar
- 100g (4oz) chilled butter, diced, plus extra for greasing
- 2 large egg yolks
- 2–3 tablespoons ice-cold water
- 1kg (2¼lb) mixed Irish apples, such as Elstar, Jonagold and Golden Delicious, peeled, cored and sliced
- 50g (2oz) caster sugar, plus extra for dusting
- 1 tbsp lemon juice
- 1 tsp ground cinnamon
- 1 egg
- chilled cream, to serve (optional)

1
Sift the flour and icing sugar into a bowl. Using a table knife, work in the butter, then mix in the egg yolks with just enough of the ice-cold water to make a dough. Wrap in clingfilm and chill for 30 minutes.

2
Preheat the oven to 190°C (375°F/ gas mark 5). Cut the pastry in half and roll one piece out on a floured work surface. Use to line the bottom of a 23cm (9in) buttered pie dish, leaving a 1cm (½in) overhang.

3
Mix the sliced apples in a bowl with the caster sugar, lemon juice and cinnamon. Put in the lined pie dish. Roll out the rest of the pastry large enough to cover the apples. Beat the egg and use to brush the edges, then lay the pastry on top.

4
Crimp the edges of the pie and roll out the trimmings to decorate. Brush with egg and sprinkle with sugar. Make small slits in the top and bake for 50–55 minutes, until golden. Serve warm cut into slices with some cream, if liked.

PEACH MELBA PANNA COTTAS

These should only be made when peaches are in season and look so pretty in the glasses. Everything can be made in advance, so they are perfect for a special celebration or even after a family barbecue.

Serves 6

- 4 large ripe peaches
- 4 gelatine leaves
- 1 vanilla pod
- 600ml (1 pint) milk
- 300ml (½ pint) cream
- 150g (5oz) caster sugar
- 4 tbsp thick Greek-style yoghurt
- 100g (4oz) fresh raspberries

1

Peel three of the peaches with a vegetable peeler. Cut the flesh off the stones and put in a blender or NutriBullet. Blend to a purée – you need about 200ml (7fl oz) in total.

2

Soak the gelatine in a bowl of water for 10 minutes to swell, then gently squeeze dry. Split the vanilla pod in half lengthways and scrape out the seeds. Put in a pan with the milk, cream and sugar. Bring to the boil, then take the pan off the heat.

3

Stir in the squeezed gelatine and peach coulis. Strain the mixture into a Pyrex jug. Cool. Once the peaches and cream mixture is cold, pour it into 6 x 175ml (6fl oz) serving glasses and put in the fridge to set for at least 4 hours or overnight is fine.

4

Remove the panna cottas from the fridge just before serving. Cut the remaining peach into slices and arrange on top with a spoonful of yoghurt and the raspberries.

RHUBARB & PLUM CRUMBLE

I think everyone in Ireland has good childhood memories of a rhubarb crumble straight out of the oven with lashings of custard. I've added in the orange as it complements the tartness of the rhubarb perfectly.

Serves 4

- 675g (1½lb) rhubarb
- 4 large ripe dark plums
- 1 vanilla pod
- juice of 1 orange
- 5 tbsp granulated sugar
- 175g (6oz) plain flour
- pinch of fine sea salt
- 75g (3oz) chilled butter, diced
- 50g (2oz) caster sugar
- chilled cream, to serve (optional)

1
Preheat the oven to 200°C (400°F/gas mark 6). Trim and cut the rhubarb into 3cm (1¼in) pieces and put in a bowl. Quarter the plums, removing the stones, and add to the rhubarb.

2
Split the vanilla pod lengthways, scrape out the seeds and add both to the fruit with the orange juice and granulated sugar. Put into a baking dish and roast for 10 minutes. Remove the vanilla pod to use again.

3
Meanwhile, to make the crumble topping, place the flour and salt into a bowl and rub in the butter until it resembles breadcrumbs. Stir in the caster sugar.

4
Lightly scatter the crumble topping over the fruit and bake for 35 minutes, until crisp and golden. Serve warm with the cream, if liked.

THE ULTIMATE GUIDE TO KITCHEN SKILLS

If you want to learn how to cook, there are a few things you might need a little help with. For example, it can take a while to learn how to use a sharp knife safely. To begin, it's best to have someone who is used to doing it help you or you could work alongside them until you know the ropes. If you're learning, think about investing in a child-friendly knife or use a small to medium-sized knife that's not too heavy. A small serrated knife is also very handy for cutting things like tomatoes. And remember, always cut away from yourself.

FOOD SAFETY IS IN YOUR HANDS!

Cooking is so much fun, but you need to keep yourself protected. Use your common sense – for instance, you'll never see me cooking in my bare feet! The first thing I do when I walk into a kitchen is put on an apron and I generally use a timer to make sure I don't forget about anything. Always get permission and follow the guidelines below to keep your kitchen a safe and happy place to work in.

1

The most important thing to remember when you start cooking is to keep the kitchen clean. The first thing I teach my young chefs is to keep their work area nice and tidy so that they can see what they're doing.

2

Keep the fridge clean and use food before its use by or sell by date.

3

Wash your hands before you start cooking and after handling meat or fish.

4

Use a separate chopping board for raw meat and fish and scrub boards after using. (Look for the Bord Bia Quality Mark to ensure it's Irish.)

5

While you're cooking, try to wash up or fill the dishwasher as you go and finish washing the rest straight after you've eaten.

6

If hand washing, use rubber gloves and hot, soapy water with a clean scrubbing brush and take care to rinse well with hot clean water. Try to leave the washing up to air-dry on the draining board. If you are using a tea towel, make sure it's a freshly washed one.

7

Use oven gloves to protect your hands and/or the work surface. Only use tea towels that are dry, as heat can pass through them quickly if they are wet.

8

Be super careful around hot pots and pans. I always put bubbling pans at the back of the cooker, turn in handles so that they are less likely to be bumped and never leave them unattended. When you've finished cooking, make sure everything is switched off properly. Leave until everything has completely cooled down, then clean the hob and cooker, ready for the next person to use.

9

Clean up splashes and spillages immediately, as they can make the floor slippery. Always make sure that mopping the floor is the last job you do before you finish.

10

Handing back a clean kitchen or just helping out to get the jobs done will mean that everyone is keener for you to keep experimenting and having fun with cooking!

HOW TOS

I was lucky that my parents, Joe and Vera, gave me a love of cooking and an appreciation of Irish ingredients from an early age. I learned by watching my mum in the kitchen prepping to get everything ready. She would often give me a job like peeling the carrots or slicing the tomatoes. I was the first boy to ever do Home Economics in my secondary school and I loved every minute of it. I soaked it all up like a sponge and particularly loved the practical side of the class.

Happily, things have changed radically and now many boys choose the subject thanks to the wonderful efforts of Home Economics teachers up and down the country. Indeed, since I opened the Home Economics classrooms in Belvedere College, a well-known boys' school in Dublin, several years ago, it has become their most popular extracurricular subject!

This is one of the reasons why I wanted to make this section a visual explanation of some of the basic kitchen skills that, learned correctly, will serve you well over a lifetime. Learning to do things the right way will save you lots of time and effort. Remember, some of these techniques, particularly the knife skills, will take time to master but practising regularly is the only way. You can use my pictures as a guide to make sure you are on the right track.

In some cases I show you the different ways to chop a particular fruit or vegetable, for example how to make carrots into batons (long sticks), which then makes them easier to finely chop, or cutting the perfect lemon wedge or cheek to garnish a dish. I really hope they encourage you to learn in a fun way and give you a love of food that stays with you forever. The aim of this section is to help you approach the recipes with confidence and understanding. There is a whole world of cooking here for you to explore and I hope these pages will be ones that you come back and visit from time to time when you need some guidance. Happy cooking!

HOW TO CHOP AN ONION

1

2

3

4

HOW TO
PEEL AND CRUSH
GARLIC

1

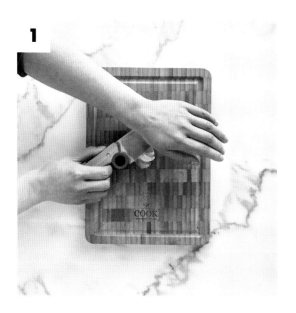

2

3

4

HOW TO
PEEL AND GRATE
GINGER

1

2

3

4

HOW TO TRIM, CHOP AND FINELY SLICE SPRING ONIONS INTO RIBBONS

1

2

3

4

5

6

7

HOW TO
CHOP A TOMATO INTO
SLICES AND WEDGES

1

2

3

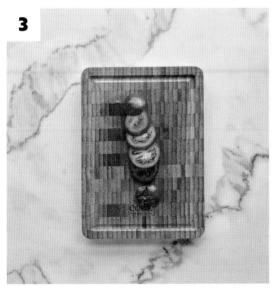

4

HOW TO
CUT LETTUCE INTO
WEDGES AND SHRED

1

2

3

4

HOW TO
CUT A LEMON INTO
WEDGES AND CHEEKS

HOW TO
SQUEEZE
A LEMON

1

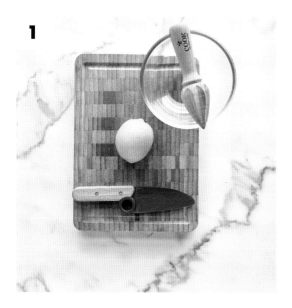

2

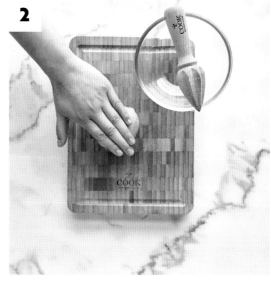

3

4

HOW TO MAKE CUCUMBER RIBBONS

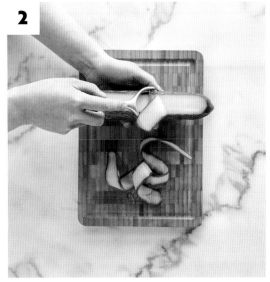

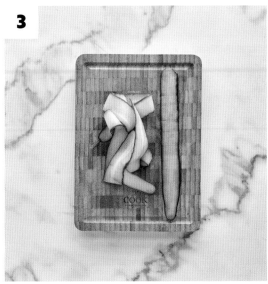

HOW TO CHOP A CARROT

1

2

3

4

5

HOW TO
CHOP
CELERY

1

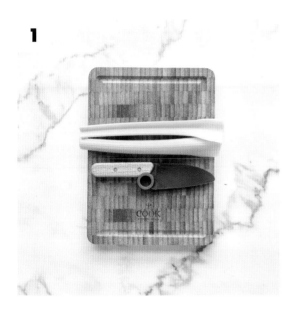

2

3

HOW TO CUT A PEPPER

1

2

3

4

HOW TO
CHOP
HERBS

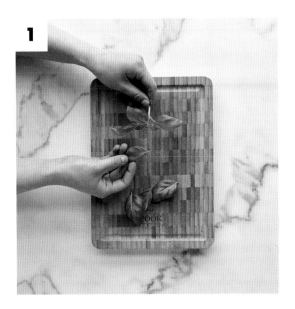

HOW TO
SAUTÉ
VEGETABLES

HOW TO
BLEND
A SOUP

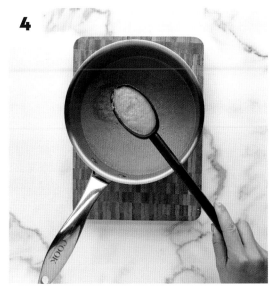

HOW TO
SEPARATE EGGS AND
WHISK TO STIFF PEAKS

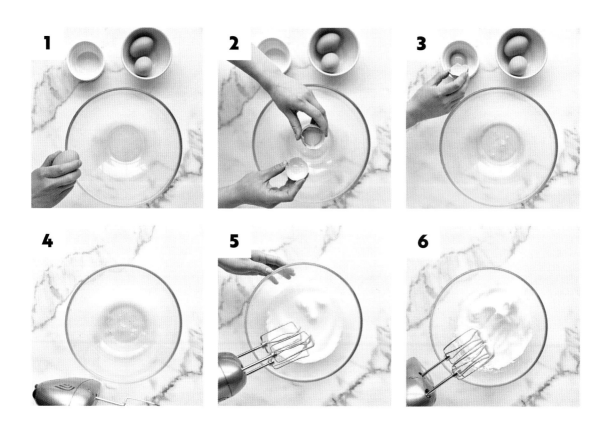

HOW TO CREAM BUTTER AND SUGAR

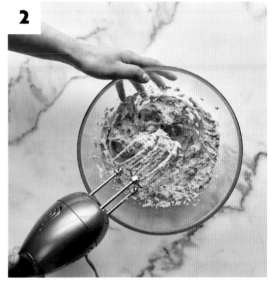

HOW TO
WHIP CREAM TO SOFT
AND STIFF PEAKS

Soft peaks

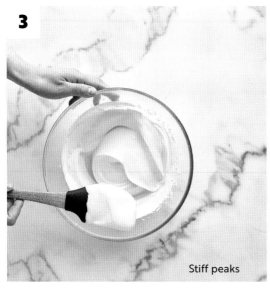

Stiff peaks

HOW TO MELT CHOCOLATE

1

2

3

4

HOW TO LINE A SQUARE TIN

1

2

3

4

HOW TO LINE A ROUND TIN

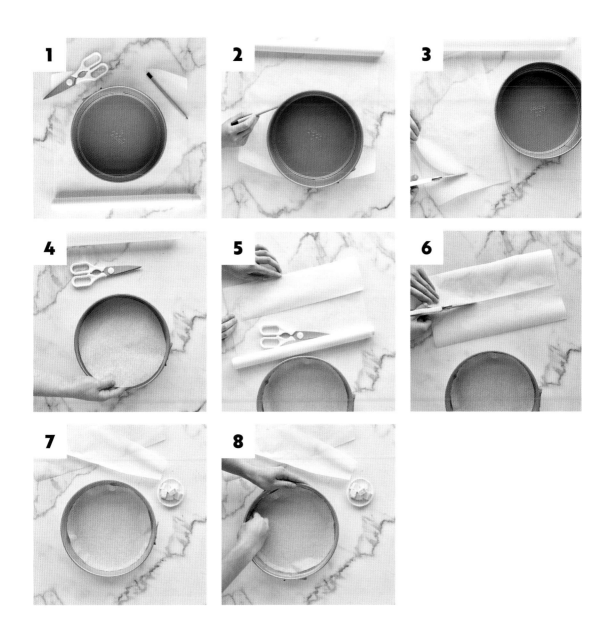

MAKE YOUR FOOD LOOK FANTASTIC

I always think visually when deciding what to cook, as the first thing we do is eat with our eyes, so I'm going to show you some tricks of the trade to make your food look as pretty as a picture! Food styling is like building a picture, so keep it simple and try to make sure it looks tasty and homemade.

Before you start, work out the composition of the shot (that means the background, napkins, glass, cutlery and perhaps putting a small dish alongside for the final flourish). Make sure all your dishes are sparkling clean and polished – a bit of kitchen paper works very well.

As a general rule, always aim for an uneven number on a plate and don't be tempted to overcrowd. If in doubt, remember that less is more – look at the final dish and see what it needs. It's much easier to add things than take them back out. Normally things that aren't too perfect and are a little higgledy-piggledy look the best.

If you're taking a picture, experiment by rotating the plate for the best angle. Take lots of options and angles so that you have plenty to choose from later. Quickly tidy up any mucky bits with cotton buds or kitchen paper, but don't worry if it looks a little messy – this is exactly what makes food look delicious. Remove all clutter from the final image so that your food can shine!

1 This is a good basic kit for food styling: water spritzer, paint brush, cotton buds, small dish of oil, tweezers, scissors, Blu Tack, sea salt flakes, freshly ground black pepper and a lemon zester.

2 Start a collection of tea towels, napkins or even nice material from fabric shops.

3 Plates with different textures and shapes can look very effective. Gather plates and bowls in the colour palettes that you like to use and keep them all together in the one place so that they are easy to find.

4 Start a collection of props by raiding your granny's house or picking things up in charity shops or house clearance or car boot sales.

5 When building your picture, small versions of things can look very cute and appetising.

6 Use different brightly coloured large (A1) pieces of paper to create instant backgrounds.

7 Sometimes showing some of the ingredients and equipment helps to build a more interesting composition.

8 Adding extra cut-out shapes to a pie makes it look more homemade.

9 Adding an extra small dish of chocolate chips to the baked cookies gives this shot more dimension.

10 Create textures with different seeds and shapes.

11 Use bowls of iced water to keep vegetables nice and crisp. This will also help them to naturally curl up.

12 Freeze Irish berries in season so that you have a stash of them to hand.

13 Use hot water to help scoop your ice cream and then refreeze before using.

14

Tie cookies with string and pop on a hand-written label.

15 Put things into little boxes or containers and hand-tie with ribbons.

16

Keep herbs on a piece of damp kitchen paper to keep them super fresh and perky.

17 Have things to hand for the final flourish – these can really help a dish to 'pop'!

18

Always wipe the edges of a plate before serving.

19 When taking a picture, keep your set-up simple and put your food on a table beside a window to get lots of lovely natural light. Turn off any overhead lights or lamps in the room.

20 Consider using filters on your phone to create great looks. There are so many apps to choose from but VSCO is a favourite of mine.

MENU THEMES

These are some simple ideas for structuring your menus. As a general rule, always consider your flavour combinations and avoid clashes, as your guests often pile a little of everything onto their plate. Choose different colours and textures for an impressive spread. Work out what space and equipment you will need to have. Make sure you have enough room to cook and store everything you need. Do as much in advance as possible – there is always plenty to do last minute without having to also worry about the food. The most important thing is to enjoy yourself – if there is one thing that life has taught me, it's to enjoy the moment.

MENU THEME: MOVIE NIGHT

1 CHORIZO CHILLI NACHOS PAGE 103

2 CHICKEN TENDERS & CHILLI COOLER PAGE 77

3 CARAMEL SWIRL BROWNIES PAGE 130

MENU THEME: PICNIC PARTY

1 SAVAGE SAUSAGE ROLLS PAGE 58

2 SALMON & PESTO RAINBOW SALAD PAGE 84

3 OATMEAL CHOCOLATE CHIP COOKIES PAGE 153

MENU THEME: FAMILY FEAST (FOR MOTHER'S & FATHER'S DAY, ANNIVERSARIES, ETC.)

1 PEPPER & PESTO PIZZA SCROLLS PAGE 64

2 BUTTERMILK SPATCHCOCK CHICKEN PAGE 108

3 WARM APPLE PIE PAGE 164

MENU THEME: COUNTRY THEMED NIGHT (MEXICAN)

1 SWEETCORN CAKES WITH SALSA PAGE 14

2 STIR-FRIED STEAK CHILLI PAGE 96

3 MANGO & STRAWBERRY ICE POPS PAGE 158

MENU THEME: BIRTHDAY CELEBRATION

MENU THEME: MIDNIGHT SLEEPOVER FEAST

1 CHICKEN SATAY WINGLETS PAGE 78

2 CHEAT'S HAM & PINEAPPLE PIZZAS PAGE 63

3 CHOCOLATE BROWNIE S'MORES PAGE 140

MENU THEME: THE GREAT OUTDOORS

1 ENERGY BREAKFAST BARS PAGE 36

2 CHICKEN TORTILLA PIES PAGE 74

3 ROCKY ROAD BITES PAGE 150

INDEX